CAMBODIA'S NEW DEAL

A Report by William Shawcross

Contemporary Issues Paper #1

CARNEGIE ENDOWMENT FOR INTERNATIONAL PEACE

Distributed by the Brookings Institution, Department 029,
Washington, D.C. 20042-0029, USA, 1/800-275-1447.

Copy editor: Stephanie Terry
Cover: Paddy McLaughlin Concepts & Design

Cover photo credit: Tim Page, Prey Veng, Cambodia
Cover depiction: *A United Nations helicopter carrying Norodom Ranariddh
leaves supporters covered in dust.*

Library of Congress Cataloging-in-Publication Data

Shawcross, William.
  Cambodia's new deal: a report / by William Shawcross.
    p. cm. — (Contemporary issues paper ; #1)
  Includes bibliographical references.
  ISBN: 0-87003-051-5 : $9.95
    1. Cambodia—Politics and government—1975- 2. Cambodia—
Economic conditions. I. Title. II. Series.
  DS554.8.S539 1994   94-15976
  959.604—dc20   CIP

The Carnegie Endowment for International Peace

The Carnegie Endowment was founded in 1910 by Andrew Carnegie to promote international peace and understanding. To that end the Endowment conducts programs of research, discussion, publication and education in international affairs and American foreign policy. The Endowment also publishes the quarterly journal *Foreign Policy*.

As a tax-exempt operating foundation, the Endowment maintains a professional staff of Senior and Resident Associates who bring to their work substantial firsthand experience in foreign affairs. Through writing, public and media appearances, congressional testimony, participation in conferences, and other activities, the staff engages the major policy issues of the day in ways that reach both expert and general audiences. Accordingly, the Endowment seeks to provide a hospitable umbrella under which responsible analysis and debate may be conducted, and it encourages Associates to write and speak freely on the subjects of their work. The Endowment convenes special policy forums and, from time to time, issues reports of commissions or study groups.

The Endowment normally does not take institutional positions on public policy issues. It supports its activities principally from its own resources, supplemented by non-governmental, philanthropic grants.

Table of Contents

Foreword

It is a tragic twist of twentieth-century history that the small, poor country of Cambodia became a killing ground, making its suffering survivors wards of the international community. Many years ago, the British journalist William Shawcross took up the burden of chronicling Cambodia's nightmare. Two books (*Sideshow: Kissinger, Nixon and the Destruction of Cambodia*, 1979, and *The Quality of Mercy: Cambodia, the Holocaust, and the Modern Conscience*, 1984) and countless articles testify to this author's rich experience and deep concern for Cambodia. Over the course of twenty years Shawcross has repeatedly visited Cambodia and its neighbors, reporting the news and describing the terrors of war and destruction.

In this brief survey Mr. Shawcross hopefully begins a chronicle of Cambodia's resurrection. The 1991 Paris peace accords, which provided for a comprehensive United Nations–sponsored settlement, initially aroused dismay among many in the West because they made the genocidal Khmer Rouge an integral part of the Cambodian political scene. The settlement also aroused suspicion in a Cambodian society conditioned to abuse by its neighbors and betrayal by its leadership. Yet, after eighteen months of U.N. administration, the Cambodian people boldly and unmistakably embraced peace. One year ago, nearly nine-tenths of registered voters cast ballots in a historic election. In the end, the war-weary people of Cambodia voted themselves a new chance, *Cambodia's New Deal*. The U.N. effort had given a nation drained of its human and physical capital a new lease on life. Moreover, China has largely turned away from Cambodia and the Khmer Rouge, and Vietnam appears finally to have folded its tents. The Khmer Rouge suffered a serious popular rebuff in the election.

The story, however, is not over. A stable Cambodian state is a long way off. The country is still badly fractured politically, economically, socially. Many of its talented people remain outside the country. Most of its infrastructure has to be rebuilt from scratch. It has little effective government, and putting one together will not be easy. Unfortunately, the Khmer Rouge are still a destabilizing force. The ability of the new government to wrest control of the battlefield is far from certain. The Royal Army is ill-equipped, poorly led, and ill-paid. The Khmer Rouge continue to receive external support.

National reconciliation is of course incomplete. Cambodia's scars are decades deep and may take generations to heal. It would take a large volume to detail Cambodia's needs, far more than this brief survey can provide. Cambodia's government is barely functioning and has been largely held together by the fading leadership of King Sihanouk. What happens to the existing coalition after Sihanouk is a matter of grave concern and uncertainty. For all his peculiarities, modern Cambodia has never been without him. As for the international community, how long will it continue to give Cambodia the tremendous help and attention it needs?

In 1993 the Carnegie Endowment for International Peace asked Mr. Shawcross to provide his own personal assessment of the country's situation and prospects. This report presents just such an intimate portrait. Shawcross vividly details the events leading to the formation of Cambodia's coalition government and paints a timely landscape of the present Cambodian scene. His insights into Cambodian history and culture lend context to this account of the last two years and a realist's perspective on the problems that a new Cambodia must confront to sustain peace. Shawcross makes a strong case for continuing international assistance to Cambodia, despite recent setbacks. The magnitude of Cambodia's task, the difficulty of building a viable government, and the long way Cambodia still has to go until it is fully restored to national life combine into an unfolding story that is likely to engage the author, and the international community, for decades.

Most of the writing was completed in the spring of this year. The views expressed are those of the author.

Morton I. Abramowitz
President

*Carnegie Endowment for
International Peace
June 1994*

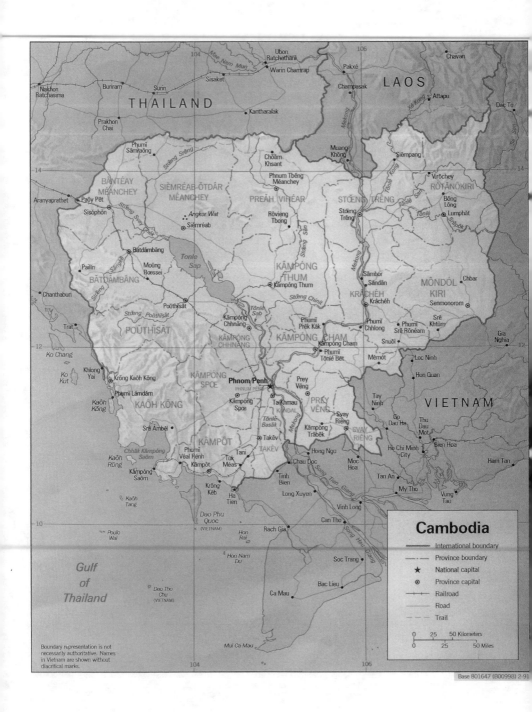

Cambodia

— International boundary
---- Province boundary
★ National capital
⊚ Province capital
+++ Railroad
—— Road
---- Trail

0   25   50 Kilometers
0   25   50 Miles

Boundary representation is not
necessarily authoritative. Names
in Vietnam are shown without
diacritical marks.

Base 801647 (B00998) 2-91

Introduction

At the beginning of 1994, Cambodia faced for the first time in almost twenty-four years the possibility of peaceful development. But by mid-1994 the prospect is still uncertain. It depends on

- the health and the good stewardship of King Norodom Sihanouk;
- the effectiveness and honesty of the new coalition government;
- the power of the Khmer Rouge and the conduct of their Thai military supporters;
- and the continued intervention and assistance of the international community.

What can be said for certain is that Cambodia has been given the best chance for peace it ever had—thanks to the overall success of UNTAC, the United Nations Transitional Authority in Cambodia, whose work began with the Paris Peace Agreement of October 1991 and ended with the adoption of a new constitutional monarchy on 24 September 1993. UNTAC was one of the largest, most intrusive, and most expensive United Nations peacekeeping operations ever. Its purpose had been to bring reconciliation, disarmament, rehabilitation and free elections, and a new, internationally recognized government to Cambodia.

It did not succeed in all particulars. Nonetheless, for Cambodia the UNTAC period was a social revolution that, with careful assistance, could transform the political landscape of the country. Chief amongst its successes was the serious blow that the U.N. presence and international persistence dealt to the strength and influence of the Khmer Rouge. With improved government and judicious foreign assistance, that would be the blow from which the brutal communist movement never recovers. Conversely, if the coalition fails to move the country, the Khmer Rouge could grow again.

National reconciliation is still far from complete. Winston Lord, the U.S. Assistant Secretary of State, pointed out on 16 June 1993 that "Much has been achieved in Cambodia, but the road ahead is perilous. . . . It will be up to those who signed the Paris Peace Accords to carry on the work which UNTAC began." As events in the year since then have shown, that is no easy task. Despite the success of the election, Cambodia needs to be rebuilt in almost every aspect of its life. The nation needs, literally, to be reconstituted and reconstructed—almost reinvented.

Cambodia today is still a semifeudal country, a place of bargaining, survival, and lawlessness. It is a state of patronage, where anyone who defies his or her patron is immediately labeled enemy or traitor. The Paris Peace Agreement presupposed something quite different: it envisioned a society in which contracts and agreements were respected. But that is hard to achieve with no independent legal system, no central authority, no tolerance, no concept of human rights or of "loyal opposition." There is only patronage and the threat of death to anyone who steps out of line—from the palace to the parish pump.

This is hardly an ideal stage on which to carry out full-scale reform. Cambodia's wish list is almost endless. If the country is to benefit in the long term from the U.N. presence, social and governmental institutions must now be developed and the beginning of a civil society nurtured and protected. The government must achieve a significant measure of security and political, economic, and social stability. Cambodians require a period of social peace for fundamental change: a time in which political dialogue can be institutionalized, human rights developed and protected, the physical environment both preserved and rebuilt, and the lives of the poor peasantry improved.

For the time being, the future of Cambodia really rests on the shoulders of the king, Norodom Sihanouk, and on the coalition government. Between them they must also find a way to deal with the Khmer Rouge, remembering that the Cambodian people voted for reconciliation over continued war.

Sihanouk has dominated Cambodian politics, with mixed results, for more than fifty years. Now, as the self-styled "father of the Cambodian people," Sihanouk has a unique opportunity and a unique responsibility: to give Cambodians the means to govern themselves. But his absences and his uncertain health have forced the fragile coalition to take central stage. Now, several months after the coalition was created, there are doubts whether it can act effectively. At the end of 1993 Sihanouk himself expressed his concern from Beijing that the new government was not acting resolutely enough in the interests of the country. In early 1994, his criticisms became fiercer and, after he returned to Phnom Penh for a few weeks, his proposed solutions became more varied.

This report examines the recent history of the country and its prospects. It explores briefly and broadly what needs to be done to consolidate the success of UNTAC. Finally, it makes a case for the continued assistance and vigilance of the international community. A final chapter, written after a visit to Cambodia in May 1994, examines the crisis that had by then developed.

Parties to the Cambodian Peace Agreement

SOC: State of Cambodia [before 1989 called *People's Republic of Kampuchea* (PRK)]

Socialist government that was installed by Vietnam in 1979 and ruled the country until 1993 with the backing of Vietnam and the former Soviet Union. The SOC, led by Hun Sen, in theory turned over control of five key ministries to the U.N. after the 1991 peace agreement, but the administrative and police structure remained largely intact. The SOC's political party, the Cambodian People's Party (CPP), came in second to FUNCINPEC in the election.

Khmer Rouge: *Party of Democratic Kampuchea*

Extremist Marxist faction led by Pol Pot that took power in 1975 and unleashed a reign of terror that killed up to 1.5 million Cambodians. Overthrown by Vietnam's 1979 invasion but fought a guerilla war with allies FUNCINPEC and KPNLF against the Vietnamese-installed government for the next decade with the backing of the United States, China, and the Association of Southeast Asian Nations (ASEAN).

FUNCINPEC: *United National Front for an Independent, Neutral, Peaceful, and Cooperative Cambodia*

Royalist faction loyal to King Norodom Sihanouk; never as militarily strong as Khmer Rouge. Won the most seats in the new parliament; Sihanouk regained the throne.

KPNLF: *Khmer People's National Liberation Front*

Pro-Western force containing some members of Vietnam War–era Lon Nol government; like FUNCINPEC, never as strong militarily as Khmer Rouge. Bitterly divided, KPNLF split into two parties before the elections, one of which (headed by Son Sann) won seats in the new parliament.

Credit: Judy L. Ledgerwood, "U.N. Peacekeeping Missions: The Lessons from Cambodia," Asia-Pacific Issues Paper No.11, March 1994. Reprinted by permission of the East-West Center, Hawaii.

CHAPTER 1

Cambodia Before the Paris Accords

Cambodia is a victim of its geography and of its political underdevelopment. Its central drama resembles that of Poland; it is a small country (some 9 million people) overshadowed by two huge and threatening neighbors—60 million Thais (Siamese) to the west, and 70 million overcrowded Vietnamese to the east. Like Poland's, Cambodia's borders have constantly changed.

Although the Cambodian people (the Khmer) have reason to fear both their neighbors, the Siamese and the Khmer share a cultural and religious Indian-influenced background. The Khmer and the Vietnamese, on the other hand, have always clashed. Cambodians fear the Vietnamese and have always believed that they seek to impose themselves upon Cambodia. Cambodian perceptions of their neighbors' ambitions still dominate the country today.

During the Angkor empire from the ninth to thirteenth centuries, the Khmer kings controlled a large part of what is now northeastern Thailand, southern Laos, and southern Vietnam. But since that empire declined, Cambodia has been prey to its neighbors. Each of them has for centuries coveted, infiltrated, invaded, and exploited Cambodia. Indeed, the country would have disappeared altogether, divided between Siam and Vietnam, if the French had not arrived and imposed a protectorate upon the moribund Cambodian monarchy in 1864.

The French prevented the growth of a strong political or even administrative class in Cambodia. They imported Vietnamese administrators and Vietnamese merchants who, together with over-seas Chinese, came to dominate the commercial and intellectual classes. At the beginning of the twentieth century, the French switched branches of the royal family, replacing the Norodom who was expected to succeed with a Sisowath. In 1941 they switched back to the Norodoms, installing the nineteen-year-old Prince Norodom Sihanouk. Today, 52 years later, at the age of 71, Sihanouk still dominates Cambodian political life just as much as does the country's geography.

By the early 1950s Sihanouk had come to understand that the best way to strengthen his own position and defuse republican sentiment was to emerge as champion of Khmer nationalism against the French. Through a skillful campaign replete with guile, bombast, threats, and feints, he succeeded in winning Cambodian indepen-dence from France in 1953.

The 1954 Geneva Conference on Indochina guaranteed Cambo-dia's neutrality and territorial integrity and called for elections. Sihanouk immediately renounced his throne in favor of his father and, as mere prince, campaigned with gusto. His semidivine appeal was irresistible and the next year he won a sweeping victory over all opponents, including those who favored republicanism. For the next fifteen years he tolerated no intermediaries, invariably insisting that he derived his legitimacy from his communion with the peasantry.

Like the French and all other Cambodian rulers before him, Sihanouk prevented an independent political class from developing in Phnom Penh. His government compelled those who returned from education abroad, usually from France, to accept the constraints of the court—which could be arbitrary and cruel. Their only alternative was to join one or the other rebel group based along the borders—the communists on the eastern border who were (mostly) supported by Vietnam, or the Khmer Serei (Free Khmer), based along the Thai border, who received help from Thailand and the United States.

Throughout the late 1950s and early 1960s, Sihanouk attempted to keep Cambodia neutral and out of the gathering storm in Indo-china. In 1965, however, after the first American combat troops had splashed ashore at Danang in South Vietnam, he broke relations with the U.S. altogether and moved towards the communists. But he predicted that if the communists won the war, he and his Cambodia would be gone forever.

American "search and destroy" missions against the communists in South Vietnam pushed them across the border into Cambodia, which at its closest is only thirty miles from Saigon. Sihanouk allowed Hanoi and the South Vietnamese National Liberation Front that it controlled to establish semipermanent base camps or sanctuaries just inside Cambodia. In 1966 Sihanouk also agreed to a personal request from Chou En-lai that military supplies for the Vietnamese communists be allowed into the port of Sihanoukville to be smuggled across the country to the communists in Vietnam.

Such abuse of Cambodia's ostensible neutrality became an increasing source of frustration to the U.S. military. Soon after President Richard Nixon was inaugurated in 1969, he authorized the secret B-52 bombing of the sanctuaries. Sihanouk made no public protest; he was already more worried about Vietnamese usurpation of the border areas.

In March 1970 Sihanouk was overthrown, while abroad, in a right-wing coup d'etat led by his prime minister, General Lon Nol, who expected—and was given—American support. In Beijing, the angry prince decided to side fully and uncritically with the North Vietnamese and the small group of Cambodian communists, whom he had hitherto fought and denigrated as *"les Khmers Rouges."*

It was a disastrous decision. Sihanouk's endorsement immediately provided the communists the nationalist appeal they could never otherwise have won. The Lon Nol regime tried to win domestic support by encouraging widespread killings of ethnic Vietnamese residents. At the end of April 1970, American and South Vietnamese troops invaded Cambodia to attack the communist sanctuaries. The war spread.

Over the next five years, Cambodia was a sideshow to Vietnam. White House policies were careless. Warfare destroyed Cambodian society and only the Khmer Rouge prospered. U.S. bombing and the growing cruelty of the Khmer Rouge combined to drive peasants off the land. Soldiers of the Lon Nol army often fought bravely but were poorly led. Corruption sapped the will of the army and the administration and alienated the people.

In April 1975, a few days before the fall of Saigon, the Khmer Rouge captured Phnom Penh. They at once began to empty the capital and all other towns and embarked on their radical, murderous revolution. They brought Sihanouk back to a deserted city and for the next three and a half years, while the people labored under harsh conditions in the countryside, they kept him under house arrest in the palace and murdered several of his children.

No one knows exactly how many people died from execution, forced labor, malnutrition, or disease under the Khmer Rouge autarchy. More than 1 million is the widely accepted estimate. The so-called killing fields display some of their remains in and around the provinces today. The regime had a strategy of sorts; it targeted the educated and trained sectors of society, Buddhist monks, and minorities—Vietnamese, Chinese, Cham Muslims, Christians, and others. It destroyed institutions, prohibited normal family life, and crushed dissent. People in some parts of the country were more harshly treated than those in others. Throughout this bloody period, the Khmer Rouge leadership enjoyed the international support of China and North Korea.

Khmer Rouge decisions were grounded in an obsessional hatred of Vietnam. While they assaulted their own people, they also carried out numerous attacks across the disputed border into Vietnam. These prompted a Vietnamese invasion at the end of 1978 that drove the Khmer Rouge out of Phnom Penh. In January 1979 Hanoi installed its own client regime, headed by defectors from the Khmer Rouge.

Khmer Rouge rule left the country and its people deeply scarred. However, the invasion—a liberation for almost all Cambodians— soon became an occupation that the Vietnamese insisted was "irreversible." Hanoi's motives were strategic rather than humanitarian; it had long nurtured ambitions of dominating an Indochinese federation. For now the Vietnamese leaders had the full support of their major ally, the Soviet Union, which had established naval bases in Vietnam at the end of the 1970s. That expansion had angered China, challenged American control of the South China Sea, and worried the noncommunist states of Southeast Asia. In 1979, the sudden presence of a large Vietnamese army close to the Thai border for the first time caused even more alarm.

In February 1979, a few weeks after the Vietnamese occupation of Phnom Penh, China launched a limited (and rather unsuccessful) punitive invasion of northern Vietnam, with Washington's tacit agreement.

Hanoi remained obdurate and the United States let the Association of Southeast Asian Nations (ASEAN) take the lead in opposing the occupation. Over the next decade Singapore spearheaded a diplomatic campaign against Vietnam and its client government. Thailand offered safe haven along its border to the Khmer Rouge and sparked the formation of noncommunist resistance groups. The international community nurtured and the Khmer Rouge recruited from hundreds of thousands of refugees who had fled to the border after the Vietnamese invasion.

Outside the Soviet bloc, almost no country recognized the regime the Vietnamese installed in Phnom Penh. At first the Khmer Rouge continued to hold the country's U.N. seat, but in 1982 they passed it to the exile Coalition Government of Democratic Kampuchea. Sihanouk led that construction, which included the three principal resistance groups: the Khmer Rouge; Sihanouk's political party, FUNCINPEC (and its Armée Nationale Sihanoukiste), and the noncommunist Khmer People's National Liberation Front (KPNLF), led by Son Sann, who had been a distinguished prime minister in the 1960s. The Chinese armed the Khmer Rouge, while the United States, Great Britain, and France helped ASEAN build up the noncommunist groups. Thailand helped all groups, but especially the Khmer Rouge. Prince Sihanouk divided his time mostly between Beijing and Pyongyang, where his "old friend" Kim Il Sung maintained a palace for him. He became a familiar figure at the U.N. General Assembly's opening sessions.

Meanwhile the regime in Phnom Penh, the People's Republic of Kampuchea (PRK), remained in limbo. Not nearly as brutal as the Khmer Rouge, it was nonetheless a hardline one-party state under rigid Vietnamese control. It tolerated no dissent, frequently torturing and even killing its opponents. It made no attempt to establish an independent judiciary and never contemplated a free press.

Its dependence on Vietnam made the regime unpopular amongst many Cambodians except insofar as it was seen as a bulwark against the Khmer Rouge. Few Cambodians returned from the diaspora to help it. Starved of U.N. or other development funds, the regime depended on aid from the Soviet bloc and India in its efforts to rebuild the educational system and to institute rudimentary health services. Production of rice, rubber, and other commodities increased, but much of the infrastructure remained utterly derelict and, indeed, it deteriorated.

In 1982 Vietnam imposed a Treaty of Friendship on Cambodia. Vietnamese citizens already enjoyed virtually unrestricted access to Cambodia. Hanoi enforced scores of border changes, almost all in its own favor, and appeared to have also removed substantial resources from Cambodia. Nonetheless, the continued occupation cost Hanoi dearly. Neither 180,000 Vietnamese troops nor Phnom Penh's army, the Cambodian People's Revolutionary Armed Forces, which came to be known as the CPAF, could quell the Khmer Rouge guerrilla campaigns. The longer Vietnam stayed, the more irksome its occupation and its client government seemed to many Cambodians. Even with its East German advisers, the Vietnamese-run secret police system was unable to prevent political infiltration by the noncommunist opposition.

In the mid-1980s, with the rise of Mikhail Gorbachev, Soviet support for Vietnam's occupation began to wane. The cost of isolation and failure to obtain wider recognition for its client became increasingly hard for Hanoi to bear. In 1986 ASEAN and Vietnam began to discuss political compromise. In November 1987 Prince Sihanouk met for the first time with Hun Sen, the former Khmer Rouge soldier whom Vietnam had installed as prime minister of the People's Republic of Kampuchea. Negotiations among the parties began in Indonesia in 1988 and then moved to Paris.

Though the talks broke down, the Vietnamese withdrew their troops just as the communist regimes in Eastern Europe collapsed in 1989. Hanoi left behind a government under Hun Sen that, while

attempting to move from a command to a market economy, was
still dogmatic, corrupt, cruel to its enemies, and (to many Cambodians) tainted by its association with Vietnam.

Although Cambodia lost much of its importance as a proxy battle-
ground with the fall of the Berlin Wall, the civil war continued.
At the end of the 1980s it seemed that the Khmer Rouge might be
able to seize more territory than they already occupied.

Senator Gareth Evans, the Australian Foreign Minister, then took
the initiative, adopting an idea put forward by U.S. Representative
Stephen Solarz to create "an international control mechanism" that
would rule Cambodia temporarily. In February 1990 Australia produced its "Red Book," the first draft of a plan for an international
peacekeeping operation in Cambodia that ultimately led to the Paris
Peace Agreement of October 1991. This was signed by nineteen
nations, including all the permanent members of the U.N. Security
Council and the ASEAN countries.

The Paris Agreement had many purposes, several of them unspo-
ken—and certainly unwritten. One was to remove an impediment
to U.S.-Soviet-Chinese detente. Another was to get the international
community off the hook of recognizing the Khmer Rouge and their
allies as the legitimate government of Cambodia. Many people
involved in the peace process expected that the elections to be held
by the U.N. would allow the legitimization of the Hun Sen regime,
perhaps in coalition with other parties. At the same time the agreement distanced the Khmer Rouge from their principal sponsor, China.
In return for allowing their Khmer Rouge clients into the political
process, the Chinese agreed to stop supplying them with weapons.
They apparently abided by their commitment. The Chinese saw
the agreement as a means of ending Vietnamese hegemony over
Indochina, restoring Prince Sihanouk to Phnom Penh, and allowing
Beijing to resume a position in Cambodia.

Including the Khmer Rouge, rather than trying them for genocide,
was at the very least a distasteful solution. It reflected Western
reluctance to stage a sustained confrontation with the Chinese and
the Thais on the issue. But, if cynical, it was also pragmatic. The
alternative was a continuation of the war, no international recogni-

tion for Cambodia, and no chance of peace. Many Western diplo-mats argued that the peace process would in itself marginalize the Khmer Rouge.

The agreement was signed by all the four Cambodian factions—the State of Cambodia (SOC—the renamed PRK), the Khmer Rouge (known as the Party of Democratic Kampuchea), Prince Sihanouk's FUNCINPEC, and Son Sann's KPNLF. The Paris peace process meant different things to each faction and events would demonstrate that they all planned to adapt or ignore parts of it.

The agreement created the United Nations Transitional Authority in Cambodia, which was to control the administration of the coun-try. Cambodian sovereignty was embodied in a Supreme National Council, which Prince Sihanouk would chair and on which all four factions would sit, and which was supposed to delegate all necessary power to UNTAC.

UNTAC: *The United Nations Transitional Authority in Cambodia*

In theory, the U.N. Security Council endowed UNTAC with wider powers than any previous U.N. peacekeeping operation. Its mandate included the supervision of a nationwide ceasefire; canton-ment and disarmament of the troops of all four factions; repatriation of 370,000 refugees from the Thai border camps; monitoring of human and civil rights; and the creation of a neutral political environment through direct control over the areas of foreign affairs, defense, national security, finance, and information. Free and fair elections would also be held for a Constituent Assembly. UNTAC was to help commence the rehabilitation and development of the country and to promote "reconciliation." The mandate was ambitious.

By early 1992 the U.N. planners had decided UNTAC would need a force of 12 infantry battalions and support units—some 16,000 men—plus 5,000 civilians. The program was expected to cost more than $1.7 billion.

The U.N. was lamentably slow in deploying UNTAC's elements and advance planning in New York was fragmented. At the beginning of 1992 fighting between the Serbs and Croats in the former Yugoslavia was already preoccupying the Secretariat. It quickly became evident that the U.N. was ill-prepared to mount such large peacekeeping operations.

Even the appointment of the secretary-general's Special Representative, Yasushi Akashi, a senior U.N. diplomat, was delayed. He arrived only in March 1992, along with the Force Commander, Australian Lieutenant General John Sanderson, and the heads of UNTAC's components, some of whom had been recruited only at the last minute.

The anticipated deployment of the 16,000 multinational troops lagged behind schedule. Sanderson directed that infantry and other line units should arrive with 60 days' supplies, so they could operate independently until external logistics support arrived. The Civilian Police and Civil Administration components of UNTAC did not take similar initiatives and, as a result, they arrived even later. Member governments of the U.N. often proved reluctant to release administrators, arguing that they themselves were short of qualified staff. Akashi later acknowledged that the U.N. must have seemed very inefficient to the Cambodian factions.

Even after the civilian administrators were finally deployed, UNTAC found itself unable to take control of the five key areas of defense, finance, foreign affairs, information, and public security, as Article 6 of the Paris Agreement demanded. In the provinces small groups of civil servants from New York or Geneva often faced entrenched, labyrinthine local administrations backed by all the resources (police included) of the party-state. Foreign officials with no experience of the country, denied direct contact by the language barrier, found it impossible to comprehend the complex patterns of family, patronage, and political relationships that made up Cambodian society.

As a result the Khmer Rouge could, with some reason, claim that the government, the State of Cambodia, was surviving Paris almost intact. According to some defectors, the Khmer Rouge leaders were at first prepared to disarm and canton their troops. But by April 1992 they had become increasingly restive. They accused UNTAC of unduly favoring the Hun Sen regime and found excuses for complaint. Nonetheless, discussions between all four factions and UNTAC continued. On 9 May General Sanderson announced that Phase 2 of the agreement, demobilization and cantonment, would begin on 13 June.

In May, as the SOC appeared increasingly confident of survival, the Khmer Rouge leadership became more unyielding and its liaison officers became less cooperative with U.N. military observers. They announced that their troops could not be demobilized under UNTAC supervision, and UNTAC could not enter the areas they controlled— unless SOC structures were completely dismantled. The Khmer Rouge have always attempted to keep their army and populations away from the "pollution" of foreigners, and the U.N.'s presence was a clear threat.

On 30 May 1992 the Khmer Rouge used a simple bamboo pole to prevent Akashi and Sanderson from transiting the Khmer Rouge area near Pailin in western Cambodia. Although the flimsy road block was not heavily defended, and the U.N. had every right to pass it, Akashi and Sanderson decided to make no such attempt.

Sanderson's then deputy, the French General Michel Loridon, wanted to call the Khmer Rouge's bluff and send U.N. troops into their areas at once. But Sanderson believed that such pressure might at once result in wider warfare. Moreover, most of the countries that had sent troops would not tolerate their use in battle against the Khmer Rouge. On a practical level, the U.N. battalions were not positioned for offensive action against the Khmer Rouge. He pointed out that UNTAC was a peacekeeping mission that could not engage in peace enforcement. His policy was much abused by laptop generals in the press corps, but any other might well have betrayed the peace process completely.

The partial cantonment of the other three factions began in June 1992, but that of the Khmer Rouge did not. After August 1992 the Khmer Rouge deliberately excluded UNTAC from their areas. Although guerrilla defectors later said they were ordered not to kill anyone from UNTAC, in some areas Khmer Rouge commanders were more intransigent than in others.

By the end of 1992 UNTAC had in effect stopped trying to pursue the comprehensive political settlement spelled out in the Paris Agreement. Instead, it attempted merely to create a new Cambodian government with domestic and international legitimacy. It had accepted a de facto reduction of the Paris mandate. A series of U.N. Security Council resolutions formally effected that change.

Meanwhile, the continuing arrival of UNTAC troops and civil administrators had an enormous impact on Cambodia's economy, especially in Phnom Penh. UNTAC's international officials were paid a per diem of $145 while the average annual income in Cambodia was approximately $160. Land values, rents, and the prices of services and utilities soared, with no commensurate increase in government wages. As a result, a double economy quickly developed and a large proportion of civil servants left their desks in order to profit from the private sector boom. In Phnom Penh inflation, corruption, and nepotism became ever more pervasive. New brothels were established and AIDS began to spread.

But in substantial ways UNTAC's presence at once began to bring great benefit to Cambodian society. That was especially true in the realm of human rights. The Human Rights Component managed to free political prisoners and others detained for long periods without trial. The use of leg irons in prisons was ended. A political spring emerged in Phnom Penh where, for the first time, free discussion and debate were encouraged. Several Cambodian human rights groups were formed, recruiting hundreds of thousands of members. Political parties proliferated. The teaching of English, strictly controlled under the previous regime, became very popular. The number of uncensored newspapers began to grow. In a state where politics had always included thuggish brutality, UNTAC's Civic Education program and Radio UNTAC, when it was finally established, taught the virtues of free speech and democratic behavior.

At the same time UNTAC's Electoral Component, working with 700 U.N. volunteers, most of them very dedicated people, managed to register a phenomenal 4.8 million voters by the end of 1992. The enthusiasm Cambodian people brought to voter registration was a welcome surprise to all UNTAC officials. Meanwhile, the U.N. High

Commissioner for Refugees conducted the repatriation of some 370,000 refugees from the Thai border, many of whom had been consigned to camps for more than ten years.

Throughout this period Prince Sihanouk was supposed to chair the Supreme National Council, but he spent large amounts of time out of the country. He visited North Korea, where poor communications kept him almost completely out of touch with Phnom Penh, and Beijing, where several meetings of the Supreme National Council actually had to be held.

At one such meeting in January 1993, Sihanouk demonstrated his management style by castigating a new FUNCINPEC member of the Supreme National Council, Sam Rainsy. The prince mocked him for his alleged political errors and even cast doubt on the state of his marriage. It was reminiscent of Sihanouk's treatment of his court in the 1960s.

When Sihanouk was absent from Cambodia, Yasushi Akashi chaired other meetings of the Supreme National Council; these were designated as "working sessions" in Phnom Penh. From Beijing Sihanouk characteristically issued constant faxes and statements, some on the poor state of his health, which, he said, required him to remain in China, and others on the poor state of Cambodia. He became increasingly critical of UNTAC and insisted that he would bring the Khmer Rouge back into government whatever the results of the "UNTACist" election. At the end of 1992 he tried to arrange for presidential elections to be held before those for the Constituent Assembly. He was supported by France, but the proposal ultimately foundered.

Altogether twenty different parties registered to compete in the election. Some U.N. officials hoped right up to the registration deadline in early February 1993 that the Khmer Rouge would return to the process, particularly after they announced the formation of their own political party. Despite several Security Council resolutions insisting that all sides comply with the Paris Agreement, the Khmer Rouge did not do so.

Instead, secure along the Thai border, the Khmer Rouge embarked on a highly profitable assault upon the environment. With the help of the Thai Army and private Thai companies, they pillaged the fabulous store of timber and gems under their control. By the end of 1992 they were thought to be making as much as $20 million a month while inflicting appalling environmental damage.

Aerial film, taken from a U.N. helicopter, shows vast areas of forest felled and topsoil ravaged, as well as large Thai camps for loggers and gem miners inside Cambodia. The U.N. refused to release the film for fear of offending the government of Thailand. Rivers became choked with mud, and fishing at the northeast corner of Cambodia's Great Lake was harmed. The Supreme National Council banned the export of logs, but the Khmer Rouge and the Thais evaded the restrictions by setting up sawmills just inside the Cambodian border so that they could export planks rather than logs.

The Khmer Rouge were not the only ones raping the forests. The Phnom Penh regime also exported large amounts of timber—to Thailand, Vietnam, and Japan. The factions continued to sell off the country's natural resources at an alarming rate and with no regard to the environmental consequences. In most instances individuals or parties—and not the state—profited.

There was escalating violence in the months leading up to the May 1993 election. The Khmer Rouge fired on UNTAC helicopters and detained UNTAC personnel sometimes for days at a time. Much worse, they continued murderous attacks upon Vietnamese residents of Cambodia, hoping to turn their presence into a major election issue. More than 100 Vietnamese civilians were murdered in different incidents. Few Cambodian politicians denounced the attacks outright, and Sihanouk advised ethnic Vietnamese to leave Cambodia for their own safety.

For its part, the SOC embarked on a policy of harassing and attacking all its political opponents, especially FUNCINPEC. The regime employed what it called "reaction forces" and "A-groups"—often vigilante thugs.

UNTAC responded with one of its bolder initiatives. Its Control Teams mounted investigations into the activities of such groups in three provinces, Prey Veng, Kompong Cham, and Takeo, managing to seize provincial government working papers and even notebooks.

Its "UN-Confidential" reports on the SOC network revealed that the regime was sabotaging and intimidating political parties wherever it could. One SOC provincial police report from Prey Veng boasted of "preventing utterly the work of other parties." It revealed: "We have assigned forces to . . . prevent [other parties'] engaging in their activities. We have broken their internal forces. . . . We have sent good forces to attack and break them in a timely manner."

SOC security forces hand-picked troublemakers in the local community to carry out attacks. One district-level document recorded the instruction, "in the work of fashioning reaction forces, aim at getting persons with foul mouths." The police were told to view all other political parties as "targets" but at the same time to "keep their hands clean"—not get caught.

After government agents killed or wounded at least 100 FUNCINPEC officials, Prince Ranariddh, the leader of FUNCINPEC and son of Prince Sihanouk, came under great pressure from within his own party, and from his former Khmer Rouge allies, to withdraw from the election. That would have destroyed the election entirely. He refused to do it.

The broadcasts of Radio UNTAC helped offset the political impact of the violence of the regime and the threats of the Khmer Rouge. The UNTAC Information Component, run by American diplomat Timothy Carney, had established the station in November 1992 over the initial opposition of U.N. Secretary-General Boutros Boutros-Ghali. It became one of the most successful components of the U.N.'s operations in Cambodia. For the first time Cambodians had a free and unbiased source of information and nearly the entire population became avid listeners. Along with UNTAC's Civic Education programs, Radio UNTAC was crucial in convincing ordinary voters that they could ignore intimidation and vote secretly. Even Khmer Rouge soldiers became loyal listeners. Independent radio may well prove essential to all U.N. peacekeeping operations.

The weeks leading up to the election of 23 May were increasingly tense for UNTAC and war-weary Cambodians. When a 20-year-old Japanese volunteer, Atsuhito Nakata, was killed in Kompong Thom province, many people feared that it marked the beginning of an all-out Khmer Rouge assault upon the U.N. workers who were so crucial to the electoral process. (Subsequently, a U.N. investigation revealed that the Khmer Rouge did not in fact carry out Nakata's murder.)

A few volunteers left in terror but most demonstrated great courage, remaining at their often isolated electoral posts in the countryside. Fears mounted when, at the end of April, the Khmer Rouge pulled their last remaining representatives from Phnom Penh. That seemed to presage attacks on Phnom Penh itself. Some UNTAC officials felt that the Paris Agreement's precondition for a "neutral political environment" did not exist, and the election should be postponed or even canceled. But that, of course, was just what the Khmer Rouge sought. Akashi and Sanderson argued that the election must go ahead and the General pledged to provide adequate security.

UNTAC officials were cheered by the obvious enthusiasm of Cambodians during the campaign. Rallies held by the Cambodian People's Party (CPP), the KPNLF, and FUNCINPEC were well attended and passed off peacefully. When the People's Party tried to interfere with FUNCINPEC's campaign, as in refusing to allow Ranariddh to fly his plane around the country, UNTAC lent him a helicopter.

On 21 May, two days before the election, two Chinese engineers serving with UNTAC were killed in a Khmer Rouge attack. The Security Council unanimously condemned the murders and also expressed its determination that the election take place as planned. By that stage, China was no longer prepared to give any political support to its former Khmer Rouge client. UNTAC's approach had succeeded in isolating the Khmer Rouge.

Sihanouk spent most of the months preceding the election in Beijing, whence he continued to alternate grudging praise and denunciations of what he called the "UNTACist" plans. He insisted that if the election was canceled, he would form a quadripartite administration including the Khmer Rouge. Khmer Rouge leaders tried to persuade him to sit out the election in China and, until the very last moment, it seemed likely that he would do so. In the week before the election he received letters urging his return from both the U.N. secretary-general and French President Francois Mitterrand. Mitterrand's request had especially strong wording. Reminding the prince that the world had invested much, including lives, in UNTAC, Mitterrand warned that no one would understand if he failed to go home and support the electoral process.

Sihanouk arrived in Phnom Penh, with his customary North Korean bodyguards, the day before the election and thereby gave the process his belated imprimatur. Some believe that his presence had a decisive effect, deterring Khmer Rouge attacks and instilling in the electorate the courage to vote. His return was a significant blow to the Khmer Rouge.

The Election and Its Aftermath

When thunder broke over Phnom Penh early on the morning of Sunday, 23 May, many people awoke fearing that it was a Khmer Rouge barrage. It was not. That morning hundreds of thousands of people arrived at ballot stations in the rain.

The political mood of Phnom Penh was epitomized by the responses awaiting first Chea Sim, the hardline former Khmer Rouge who was chairman of the People's Party, and then Prince Ranariddh when they arrived at the Olympic stadium to vote. Chea Sim was watched in silence by thousands of voters; Ranariddh was given a rapturous welcome. FUNCINPEC easily won Phnom Penh.

Throughout the country people flocked to the polls in their best clothes. U.N. volunteers and Cambodian electoral workers checked their U.N.-issued ID cards, dipped their fingers in indelible invisible ink, and handed the voters a large folded ballot paper with the symbols of the 20 participating parties. Voters went behind the cardboard booths, made their marks, and often came out smiling. (Despite Cambodia's high illiteracy rate, the number of invalid papers was remarkably low—only about 4 per cent.)

This author has rarely seen anything so moving as the joy with which ordinary Cambodians defied violence and intimidation and grabbed the opportunity the world gave them to express their wishes. Recalling Shakespeare's *Henry V*, a reporter for the English language paper the *Phnom Penh Post* called the election Cambodia's Crispin Day. And so it was.

Nonetheless, the government's influence was clearly felt. In some areas turnout was high because government officials ordered people to vote. In some districts officials allegedly gave voters money to vote for the People's Party. In others people were reportedly forced to take elaborate and fearsome oaths that they would do so.

In Kompong Cham Prime Minister Hun Sen was a candidate for the CPP and enjoyed the support of his brother, the notably corrupt governor. The regime had divided the population into groups of ten, one party member controlling each group and responsible for getting them to the polls, ordering them how to vote as they went in, and interrogating them as they came out. After the results were announced, however, it became clear that thousands upon thousands of those people who had been bullied by the regime had in fact voted for FUNCINPEC. Kompong Cham went to FUNCINPEC.

In some areas Khmer Rouge officers warned people that to vote would be to commit suicide. Before the election Khieu Samphan, the Khmer Rouge president, had insisted that no one would take part in what he called "this stinking farce." His speech was repeated on Khmer Rouge radio throughout the election. After the voting began Khmer Rouge radio claimed that no one was going to the polls. As it became clear that the turnout was enormous, the radio was forced to acknowledge higher numbers—but never the truly startling figure of 90 per cent turnout nationwide. Indeed, in one of his letters to Sihanouk, Khieu Samphan actually protested that such a high turnout was impossible. UNTAC officials would have been happy if 75 per cent of the electorate had turned out to vote, but the overwhelming response represented a ringing endorsement of the process and a serious rebuff to the Khmer Rouge.

The relative peace of the election came as an astonishing, welcome surprise. Theories abound as to why the Khmer Rouge did not attack. Some military analysts argue that they did as much as they could, and that their inaction reflected above all the logistical and manpower constraints upon them. General Sanderson believed that UNTAC's battalions and CPAF, the government forces, had, in much of the country, managed to push the Khmer Rouge back from the main areas of population and polling.

Some Khmer Rouge defectors later said that a few days before the election, they had been instructed to cancel the planned attacks. Others in Kompong Thom province told journalist Nate Thayer of the *Phnom Penh Post* that their orders were to attack throughout the election. There was clear disarray. Perhaps the leadership finally decided that it could not enforce a complete boycott of the election, and believed that a victory by the Phnom Penh regime was not inevitable. Towards the end of the election week, as the massive size of the national turnout became obvious, some Khmer Rouge commanders in the northwest even trucked their people to the polls, where they presumably voted for FUNCINPEC.

Other intelligence reports assert that the Khmer Rouge's few allies—in the Thai and Chinese leaderships—warned them against destroying the election. The international community had invested so much that disruption would elicit such international obloquy that they could never have any hope of being included in any future coalition government.

Regardless of the Khmer Rouge's reasons for restraint, their bluff had been called. Both the international community and the Cambodians had withstood their threats against the election.

On Saturday, 29 May, after polling ended, Yasushi Akashi declared UNTAC satisfied that the elections were free and fair. At a Supreme National Council meeting chaired by Prince Sihanouk at the palace that morning, FUNCINPEC promised to accept the results, whatever they were. But, speaking for the People's Party, Hun Sen refused to offer any such assurance.

After the ballot counting began on 29 May, Radio UNTAC began to broadcast rolling totals of the votes as counted. The count went much slower than hoped. But by Tuesday, 1 June, it appeared that the ruling People's Party would not win even a plurality of seats in the new Assembly.

To the former Khmer Rouge who controlled the CPP and the regime in Phnom Penh, defeat was unthinkable. They began to threaten more widely. A group of government soldiers arrived to menace one provincial vote counting center. The U.N. strengthened its defenses at all of them. Spokesmen for the regime denounced Radio UNTAC;

the U.N. reinforced the security around the station. Phnom Penh officials inveighed against alleged irregularities in the election and warned that unless it was held again in four provinces, they would not accept the results. They said they expected public insurrections and mutinies that they could not control. They warned that the army and police had been asked to take "preventive measures."

When the final results were declared, the Cambodian People's Party leaders found that intimidation had won them only 38 per cent of the vote, whereas FUNCINPEC had 45 per cent. In provinces like Kompong Cham where the intimidation was most serious, the people were most defiant. The eighteen or so smaller parties were virtually wiped out; the Buddhist Liberal Democrats (BLDP, the renamed party of Son Sann) gained 3.8 per cent of the vote. In terms of seats in the new Constituent Assembly, FUNCINPEC had fifty-eight, the People's Party fifty-one, the BLDP ten, and a fourth party, Moulinaka, one. Over most of the country, people had voted for peace, for reconciliation, for Sihanouk, and, perhaps above all, for change. It was a lot to hope for.

Power in Cambodia had never before been peacefully transferred as the result of free and fair elections. As soon as the unexpected results became known, there was a clear danger that the leaders of the People's Party would invoke the old, brutal traditions. The intense internecine maneuvering that followed illustrates the still-traditional nature of politics in Cambodia.

Establishment of the New Government

Under the Paris Agreement, UNTAC's mandate was to end with the adoption of a new constitution and the formation of a new government by the Constituent Assembly within three months of the election. The Paris Agreement did not, unfortunately, have much to say about the period of transition.

Annex 3 Paragraph 1 of the agreement stated merely that within three months of the election the Constituent Assembly shall complete its task of drafting and adopting a new constitution "and transform itself into a legislative Assembly which will form a new Cambodian Government."

This brevity was commendable and perhaps, in view of Cambodia's tortuous political processes, wise. It did not, however, leave UNTAC with much guidance. Up until the end of May 1993, UNTAC personnel were understandably preoccupied with the election. Many had also assumed that the People's Party would win.

At the time of the election, the Australian government had prepared one of the few documents addressing the problems of transition. That paper examined the continuing internal security problem, a collapsed economy and dilapidated infrastructure, an inefficient and under-resourced administration, a lack of trained middle management, a limited set of options for raising revenue, a near-total breakdown in law and order, and a police force and ill-paid army suffering from low morale and equipment deficiencies. All of those areas required action by the new government, but the paper suggested that the international community attempt to help alleviate the situation.

First and foremost the question of political power had to be resolved. UNTAC was left very much a bystander as the political parties and Sihanouk himself seized the initiative. Those plots and subplots that did not revolve around him centered on two of his sons, Ranariddh, the victorious leader of FUNCINPEC, and his half brother, Prince Chakrapong, who defected from FUNCINPEC in 1992 to become a member of the CPP Politburo and Deputy Prime Minister in the Hun Sen regime. He was known to have made a fortune through his corrupt interests in aviation and other businesses. He was also rumored to be closer to Sihanouk's wife, Princess Monique, than was Ranariddh. The only certainty, however, was that the two brothers loathed each other.

As soon as the voting trends became clear, rumors began to circulate that army generals and hardline communists in the administration were organizing a coup. On 31 May a brace of Phnom Penh generals went to the palace to warn Prince Sihanouk of what might happen; Sihanouk did not see them, but Princess Monique did. Government spokesmen denounced election "irregularities," but those were in

fact inconsequential. The next day Chea Sim, the People's Party
leader, visited Sihanouk and asked him to negotiate a compromise
with Ranariddh, but Ranariddh had left Phnom Penh saying he feared
for his life.

On 3 June both Chea Sim and Hun Sen went to the palace and
asked Prince Sihanouk to assume absolute power. They warned of
violence against FUNCINPEC. Sihanouk responded with characteristic
panache—by announcing the formation of a "National Government
of Cambodia," with himself as head of state, prime minister, and
supreme commander of the armed forces and police and with
Ranariddh and Hun Sen as deputy premiers. This occurred well before
the vote counting ended.

Sihanouk made the proposal without consulting Ranariddh, his
son and the winner of the election. Ranariddh, now in his headquarters at Ampil in northwest Cambodia, was furious. He sent a fax to
his *"Papa très Venere,"* expressing his great surprise at Sihanouk's
plan. He said he would find it difficult to work with Hun Sen and
the People's Party "assassins" who had attacked, vilified, and killed
FUNCINPEC officials during the election. He also refused to work with
his half-brother Chakrapong "who holds no other thought than to
eliminate or to kill me. . .or to apply a Burmese-style solution." Until
the People's Party unequivocally accepted the results of the election,
no cooperation was possible. By now the Khmer Rouge themselves
were making similar demands—with no sense of irony.

Ranariddh was not alone in viewing Sihanouk's proposed new
government as an attempt by Hun Sen and his hardline colleague
to remain in power behind the fig leaves of Sihanouk and FUNCINPEC.
U.N. officials in Phnom Penh described Sihanouk's action as an
attempt at a constitutional coup and a violation of the Paris Agreement. To complicate matters, the U.S. mission privately criticized
the plan while the French mission supported Sihanouk's initiative
and promptly leaked information about the American position. That
aroused Sihanouk's longstanding distrust of the United States.

Infuriated by the criticism, Sihanouk tore up his plan and on 4
June said that Ranariddh and the Hun Sen regime would now be
responsible "for whatever bloody and tragic events that could happen

to our hapless country and unfortunate people." He also attacked UNTAC for its "colonialism." The next day he broadcast a further rebuke to Ranariddh, urging him to change his mind. "If you give power to Sihanouk, all problems will be solved. I propose to establish a transitional government, to bring Cambodia from insecurity to a bright future of peace."

He complained about the conditions that FUNCINPEC was laying down. Although he said "Papa is not angry with his child," he warned that everyone should remember that Ranariddh had used Sihanouk's name to win the election. Finally, on the advice of his astrologer, he said he would delay any further plans to form a new government until his birthday in October.

The People's Party kept up the pressure. In what was a piece of theater—a frightening one—Sihanouk reported to the Supreme National Council on 10 June that his son Chakrapong and the People's Party Interior Minister Sin Song had left Phnom Penh to establish an "autonomous zone" in the eastern provinces of Prey Veng, Svay Rieng, and Kompong Cham. Two days later the provinces of Stung Treng, Ratanakiri, Mondolkiri, and Kratie, all in eastern Cambodia, were said to have seceded.

The "autonomous zone" had a serious purpose. The SOC unleashed its "A-group" and "reaction force" thugs. They smashed local offices of UNTAC, of FUNCINPEC, and of other parties opposing the CPP. FUNCINPEC and KPNLF workers were threatened, many were badly beaten, and some were murdered. About 4,000 people fled to Phnom Penh—and others went to Khmer Rouge areas. Demonstrations took place against UNTAC itself and on 12 June Sihanouk demanded UNTAC's withdrawal from the area. UNTAC did evacuate some civilian staff but left its military and civilian police in place. Many of them were terrified and did little to help, but the Indian battalion serving with UNTAC in Kompong Cham remained calm and prevented the situation from degenerating further.

The People's Party clearly used the episode to blackmail both FUNCINPEC and UNTAC in an attempt to reverse the election results. At the same time, however, a gap emerged between Phnom Penh's army, CPAF, and its political leadership. On 10 June the Armed

Forces General Staff, under pressure from General Sanderson and
some of the donor embassies, agreed to form a national army
and announced its support for whatever government emerged from
the elections.

On 13 June Ranariddh, who may have had real reason to fear for
his life in Phnom Penh, returned to the city. UNTAC's initial reactions
were weak; it reminded the Phnom Penh regime of its responsibility
to keep order and declared that the announcements of secession
were "in violation of international law, the territorial integrity of
Cambodia and the Paris Peace Accords."

The Constituent Assembly met for the first time on 14 June and
in an almost surreal first act, declared null and void the March 1970
overthrow of Prince Sihanouk. The Assembly thus expunged the act
of *lese majeste* that had obsessed Sihanouk for twenty-three years.
Recognizing him as true head of state through all the travails since
1970, it endowed him with unspecified "full and special powers."

In an indication of his management style, Sihanouk announced
at the 14 June meeting that he was inviting members to meet *"en
famille"* at the palace with "Papa." They met in the palace throne
room the next day in a politico-religious atmosphere reminiscent of
the old days of monarchy. Monks presided and incense burned on
the altar. Sihanouk invoked the spirits (*tevodas*) to witness the
gathering; he said members should leave behind bad feelings of the
past and commit themselves to working together peacefully.

On 15 June the CPP's secession ploy effectively ended with the
temporary flight of Chakrapong to Vietnam—which had given the
secessionists no help. Indeed, unlike its former client Vietnam had
already accepted the election results. No punishment awaited the
secessionists. When they returned to Phnom Penh, Sihanouk received
Chakrapong, Sin Song, and Hun Sen to thank them for obeying
his order to end the secession. Sihanouk subsequently promoted
Chakrapong to the rank of four-star general in recognition of his
"services" to the state.

Though the attempted secession was merely an elaborate blackmail,
it worked. FUNCINPEC now realized that it would have to compromise
with the People's Party if it was to gain any part of power by peaceful

means. The reality of the emerging deal became apparent on 16 June when Sihanouk broadcast an announcement that a "Provisional National Government of Cambodia" would be formed at once. The interim government would run Cambodia until the constitution was approved. Sihanouk would serve as head of state with two co-prime ministers, one from FUNCINPEC and one from the CPP.

Sihanouk also requested that General Sanderson become Supreme Commander of the new Cambodian Armed Forces. After Sanderson politely declined, Sihanouk agreed to take the position himself.

On 18 June Sihanouk hosted a gathering at the palace for visiting senior officials of the Core Group of nations involved in the Paris Peace Agreement. He went on to say that he was neither the tyrant nor the dictator that he was by then being painted. He insisted that all he wanted to do was establish a parliamentary system. In a dig at what he perceived to be U.S. interference, he said that while he admired the United States, he knew Latin America well—that there were many banana republics there and that he did not think Cambodia should become one, though it did have bananas. He made clear that Cambodia would accept UNTAC's advice on the new constitution, but it was essentially a Cambodian matter. In acknowledging that he had compelled FUNCINPEC to share power with the People's Party, he said it was essential to avoid civil war—the CPP had threatened to make the whole country secede. Then he would have been left with only the palace and would have had to ask Kim Il Sung for more bodyguards, he said.

Speaking at the palace session on behalf of the Core Group, Jean David Levitte, the senior French official present, insisted that all the Cambodian parties accept the result of the election, which had now been endorsed by the Security Council. He made the threat clear; the world would not give any further aid to support Cambodia unless the People's Party abided by the Paris Agreement. Three days later the People's Party at last began to move towards accepting the election result—though not the logic of its defeat.

Meetings continued into the evening, around celebrations of Princess Monique's birthday. Believing that the CPP would never hand over full power, Ranariddh agreed without enthusiasm to accept the conceit that the election had produced "no winners and no losers" and accepted parity with the People's Party in the provisional administration. He agreed that there should be both co-prime ministers and also co-ministers of defense and interior. The division of portfolios came to follow Sihanouk's suggestion: 45 per cent FUNCINPEC, 45 per cent CPP, and 10 per cent BLDP—the CPP obtaining twelve ministries, FUNCINPEC eleven, BLDP three, and Moulinaka one. The Constituent Assembly then endorsed the provisional administration.

The new arrangements did not reflect the true margin of FUNCINPEC's election victory. Some FUNCINPEC officials and members were aghast that Ranariddh had conceded so much. But the compromise aptly reflected the administrative, military, and even financial muscle of the CPP.

In a sense, that transfer amounted to a restoration of the status quo ante 1970. Sihanouk resurrected the appurtenances of the ancien regime. The new national anthem and flag were in fact old— they were the monarchist emblems of the 1960s, which, in memory at least, had been peaceful.

Sihanouk has never been one to mince words. And at the end of June, in his palace in Phnom Penh, the same palace in which the Khmer Rouge had kept him under house arrest, Sihanouk assailed the People's Party for blackmailing him into cooperation. He said to this writer that the People's Party oppressed, intimidated, and murdered people and served as "a champion of corruption," and he blamed its members for trying to protect their own interests rather than those of Cambodia. They had given an ultimatum to FUNCINPEC, saying, "If you don't share power, there will be secession and civil war."

Blackmail or not, Sihanouk believed that after 23 years of suffering and destruction he had no choice. Under pressure he even agreed that all votes in the new Assembly be passed by a two-thirds majority— ensuring that the CPP maintained its grip on government business. Fearing the alternative, a battle with the CPP, he rationalized, "We will now have stability with the CPP. Without the concessions I have made, we would have had two civil wars—one against the Khmer Rouge and one against the regime."

He also responded with gusto to recent requests from Khieu Samphan for a Khmer Rouge role: "They said in their last letter they
were not interested in being in the government. They would like to
remain simple citizens. Very dangerous! You know, I think it is
better for us all to have them in the government than to have them
as simple citizens! The simple citizens of the countryside or Phnom
Penh are nice, but the simple citizens of the Khmer Rouge, that's
another matter!"

Sihanouk expressed concern over U.S. opposition stated by the
American Assistant Secretary of State Winston Lord to inclusion
of the Khmer Rouge in any new government. His choices were limited.
"When you go into a restaurant and are given a big menu," he said,
"you can choose many different specialities. But I have a big menu
with only one dish!" He had toyed with the idea of creating a
Senate or Council to which he could appoint members and on which
the Khmer Rouge could have seats. That device would bring them
back into the national community without actually giving them a
part in government. If they refused to accept that, then he would
simply leave them in their zones with semi-autonomy. "I have no
choice," he insisted. "The other choice is to restart the war. Our
people do not deserve a war. We have to concentrate on rebuilding
the 85 per cent of Cambodia which is in our hands, before thinking
of the reunification of the country. We can't fight them. We would
not win such a war."

In mid-July, Sihanouk left Phnom Penh to spend two months in
Pyongyang (where he planned to make a film, his favorite pastime),
and Beijing, where he would have medical checkups. His departure
evoked dismay amongst those in Phnom Penh who deemed his
continued brokerage essential. Others feared that the political atmosphere of Kim Il Sung's North Korea would hardly encourage his
democratic spirit. Sihanouk said that he had to leave Cambodia
because his wife's astrologer insisted that he might be assassinated
if he remained in Phnom Penh at that time. The prince consults
closely with his wife; she consults closely with her astrologer.

During his absence from Cambodia, the Interim Coalition government functioned surprisingly well, at least on the surface and at the

upper level. The People's Party retained control of all the provinces, even those it had lost in the election; the police remained firmly in the hands of its hardliners, and in many ministries personnel and policies remained unchanged.

In one key area, however, important changes were made. Under the supervision of UNTAC's military component, the armies of the three new partners began the difficult process of amalgamation.

Meanwhile, the Khmer Rouge continued to demand a role in the new government, and in July and August they stepped up their murderous attacks on Vietnamese and on such civilian targets as trains.

In early August Ranariddh held talks with Khieu Samphan in Bangkok but made no progress. Khieu Samphan complained that nothing had changed in Phnom Penh since 1979, and Khmer Rouge radio asserted that the new government had two heads and one Vietnamese body. When Khieu Samphan declared that the Khmer Rouge had to attack Vietnamese because UNTAC had failed to remove them from Cambodia, it was depressingly clear that nothing in Khmer Rouge ideology had altered.

Ranariddh was not pleased and publicly warned the Khmer Rouge against trying to poach territory held by the elected government. On 18 August the new combined army attacked Khmer Rouge positions in several provinces. That marked a huge change: the Khmer Rouge's former allies (FUNCINPEC and the KPNLF) were now fighting with their old enemy (the CPP) against the Khmer Rouge. Close to the Thai border, they captured the important Khmer Rouge base of Phnom Chat. Many Khmer Rouge fled into Thailand, evidently receiving support from some Thai authorities.

Ranariddh broadcast over both Radio UNTAC and the official government channel an appeal to all Khmer Rouge soldiers to lay down their arms. He promised defectors that they would be integrated into the new army. By early October almost 2,000 Khmer Rouge soldiers were thought to have responded to that appeal—out of an estimated 10,000 total fighting strength. Many said they no longer saw any purpose in fighting; they had hoped that the Paris Agreement would bring peace and they had hoped to take part in the election. They did not believe their leaders' claims that they were fighting Vietnamese; the only bodies they ever saw were Cambodian, and they wanted to go home.

During that period, and after some argument amongst the donor countries as to the precedents and the proprieties, UNTAC launched Operation Paymaster, a scheme whereby the United Nations helped provide the funds for the provisional administration to pay salaries of active soldiers and civil servants. UNTAC hoped thereby to give the absurdly underpaid officials and soldiers some stake in the new political process and thus lend it stability. The program was a success and enabled both UNTAC and the interim government to determine for the first time the exact strength of the combined armed forces— some 128,000 men.

Meanwhile, a thirteen-member committee of the Constituent Assembly continued to draft a constitution in conditions of almost total secrecy. UNTAC offered support and advice, but it was rejected. At the end of August UNTAC was finally allowed to see a draft, which appeared to give undue power to the chief of state and too little protection to the rights of citizens and foreign residents of the country. Also missing were provisions for an independent judiciary and the specific prohibition of torture. UNTAC submitted suggestions, and some were accepted.

The secrecy surrounding the drafting process was disappointing. However, UNTAC's success in cultivating greater political freedoms was demonstrated by some of Cambodia's new indigenous human rights groups, led by one called Ponleu Khmer, a Citizen's Coalition for the Constitution. They felt bold enough to criticize the draft constitution publicly. Of especial concern to them were the great powers given to the head of state—who would inevitably be Sihanouk. A few months earlier, such boldness would have been unthinkable.

At the beginning of September, as the deadline for the Assembly's debate of the constitution approached, Sihanouk sent conflicting signals home as to what he really sought—the crown or merely the office of Head of State. In a letter dated 31 August from North Korea, he said that if the Assembly insisted on making him king, he would accept the honor. But on 4 September he asked the Assembly to renounce any such idea. He wrote that Cambodia had many problems to resolve, especially that of the Khmer Rouge. He believed that the controversy of a monarchy would only create new problems, writing, "We have already found the ideal formula: Cambodia is an independent, neutral and non-aligned state, neither a Kingdom nor a Monarchy. It is simply a Cambodian Cambodia."

That same day he sent a furious message to Akashi, complaining that UNTAC officials had informed the BBC that he was demanding the restoration of the monarchy. He railed at UNTAC for its "anti-Sihanoukists" who constantly frustrated his efforts on behalf of the country. He wrote that he was breaking all relations with UNTAC and asked Akashi to cancel his visit to Beijing on 10 September. After a conciliatory response from Akashi, however, relations were restored later that same day and Akashi did visit the prince in Beijing a week later.

Sihanouk expanded his vision of his role in the next few days. He faxed replies to questions sent from a newspaper, the *Cambodia Daily*, saying that he would be a king "who will reign and not govern." He emphasized that "in order to avoid civil war and secessions," the new permanent government must retain both Ranariddh and Hun Sen as co-prime ministers. (Ranariddh had been arguing that once the interim period was over, he should be sole prime minister.) The constitution, he promised, "will be one of the most liberal in the world, with a multiparty system, a market and free enterprise economic system, a clear separation of powers (legislative, executive and judiciary), an independent judiciary, an absolutely free press without any censorship, and the free circulation of books and other publications." And Cambodia, he pledged, "will become one of the most advanced democracies in the Third World, the total opposite of the Khmer Rouge Polpotism which wanted Cambodia to be the most 'advanced Communist state in the world.' "

In the first week of September, a large delegation of People's Party and FUNCINPEC deputies, led by Ranariddh and Hun Sen, flew together to Pyongyang to see Sihanouk. They carried two draft constitutions, one for a republic and one, very similar, for a constitutional monarchy. Many of them believed that despite the reservations he had recently expressed, Sihanouk did want to become king. They were right; after some discussion, he and the delegation agreed on the monarchy.

Then came a different sort of crisis. Sihanouk sent another fax, on 9 September, to say that his Chinese doctors had discovered a small tumor "in my rectum. . .not far from the anus." He would need detailed examination and treatment; he could not come back to Cambodia in September as planned, but hoped to return in October.

In his absence a five-day debate on the constitution opened in the Assembly. Outside, about 600 monks, nuns, and civilians marched in a demonstration organized by the human rights group Ponleu Khmer to demand open discussion of the constitution. Inside, the debate was surprisingly spirited and was broadcast on radio and television to widespread interest. While deputies quickly agreed to restore the monarchy, the main source of contention was whether a two-thirds majority should be required to pass all legislation. The People's Party demanded it, in order to ensure that it continued to hold the balance of power. The People's Party also insisted that the system of two prime ministers be preserved. Although FUNCINPEC resisted both demands, the People's Party had its way.

Matters were further complicated when the People's Party itself split. According to some reports, the hardline chairman of the party, Chea Sim, realized that the FUNCINPEC-led government would gradually transfer party assets to the state and thus undermine his source of patronage and power. He tried to have Hun Sen replaced as coprime minister with one of his closer proteges. Hun Sen threatened to form a new party if that were done. The specter of secession was raised once again, but it receded.

On 20 September Sihanouk announced that he might have cancer of the prostate, but he returned briefly to Cambodia a few days later. He flew into Phnom Penh on a North Korean jet provided by Kim Il Sung and was welcomed with garlands and flowers. Standing beneath a golden parasol he described the constitutional monarchy as similar to that of Great Britain. "The King reigns but does not rule," he said. He announced that in future both China and Japan would be paying his costs—he would therefore not be a burden to the Cambodian people.

He had refused an elaborate celebration on grounds of cost, and on 24 September he signed the new constitution and, in a simple but ancient ceremony, took the oath of office in the throne room of the palace. By his side was his wife Monique, who was invested as queen, thus guaranteeing her a position in Cambodia after his departure. Buddhist monks intoned prayers, servants beat a gong, and the once and future king dabbed lustral water behind his ears, bowing and beaming to all the audience. Amongst the spectators at the palace were former Khmer Rouge soldiers who had recently defected. Sihanouk embraced them while Prince Ranariddh said, "There are no more red or yellow Khmers. There are just Khmers."

It was, by any standards, an extraordinary moment and a remarkable achievement for Sihanouk. It came fifty-two years after his first coronation under French rule in 1941. Since then, Sihanouk had been king, chief of state, prime minister, political leader, musician, cineaste, magazine editor, and exile. He had at times infuriated and horrified his friends and enemies alike. He had been vain, petulant, autocratic, and unpredictable, finding it hard to tolerate dissent and treating Cambodian politicians and foreign statesman as flunkies. He had sometimes made catastrophic errors, misjudging events and his own power to influence them.

Nonetheless, he had also demonstrated an acute intuition for the popular political will and had acted with astuteness, displaying both charm and tenacity. His principal and interrelated ambitions had been to protect Cambodia from further encroachment by its neighbors and to preserve his own political power and place in history. Whatever irritation he aroused abroad, in Cambodia he was still viewed by millions of people as he saw himself, as "the father of the nation." As such, his real task was to prepare the country for his departure.

On the weekend of 26 September, General Sanderson and Yasushi Akashi left the country. The Khmer Rouge radio denounced Akashi, declared that UNTAC had brought nothing but AIDS to Cambodia, and asked the Cambodian people to "throw feces" at Akashi as he left. Instead, Akashi and Sanderson left to widespread praise.

UNTAC had by no means achieved everything that the Paris Agreement had mandated, but it had in effect conducted a brief, profound, and very welcome social revolution. "Cambodia," said Akashi, with some hyperbole, "is a striking demonstration to the world that an intractable conflict can be resolved and seemingly irreconcilable views can be reconciled. Cambodia will thus stand as a model and a shining example for other U.N. member states."

Model or not, the successes of UNTAC were both real and fragile. When the United Nations struck its tents, Cambodia still lacked security, a viable economy, and a civil society. It was still a heavily armed and fractured country. What it now needed was concerted action by the coalition government, coupled with continued international attention, to ensure that the achievements of the UNTAC period were built upon and not squandered.

CHAPTER 2

The New Politics

At the end of 1993, the prospects for Cambodia were far better than they were at the start of any year since 1970. There was an internationally recognized government committed to reform and rural development. The Khmer Rouge were weaker than at any point in the last twenty years. Much depended on whether an effective government could be established in Phnom Penh.

People in Phnom Penh seemed more relaxed than before the election. The riel had doubled its value against the dollar and was stable. Food prices had fallen—though not by as much as they should have, given the strength of the currency. Trade was flourishing. There was a sense of growing business confidence.

The departure of UNTAC had been welcomed widely, even by those (members and supporters of FUNCINPEC) who had benefited most obviously from it. Perhaps it is the fate of even successful U.N. missions to incur the resentment of those they assist.

But the country still faced enormous problems and there were already grounds for concern that the new government was failing to take advantage of the momentum and the promises of the election. FUNCINPEC had not seized the levers of power. Corruption was, if possible, increasing, and crime and violence were omnipresent.

In Cambodia today the very culture is one of lawlessness. A process of illicit revenue extraction tears at every level of society. The borders are in the control of warlords stealing the country's resources. Many roads are blocked by government soldiers or former soldiers acting as bandits and destroying legitimate commercial activity.

Soon after the new Minister of Finance, Sam Rainsy of FUNCINPEC, took office, he was shot at—apparently because he had started to reform the customs service and centralize the collection of taxes. In September bandits boarded a rubber barge on the Mekong, murdered everyone aboard, and sailed on to Vietnam where they sold the rubber for tens of thousands of dollars. In January Rainsy was forced to send his family abroad for a brief period because of death threats brought on by his anticorruption drive.

Everywhere, Cambodia is a society of patronage and theft. A district chief in the central province of Kompong Speu makes a personal fortune selling a mountain to the Thais for quarrying. Phnom Penh troops attack Khmer fishermen on a river in the remote northeastern province of Ratanakiri because the troops had leased the fishing rights to the Vietnamese. The governor of Stung Treng sells off national timber to Laos and facilitates other kinds of cross-border traffic for his own profit.

In the province and port of Koh Kong, on Cambodia's coast close to the Thai border, the Governor, Rung Phlam Kesan, has been running the province, in the words of UNTAC officials, for the benefit of his own family and that of his superiors in Phnom Penh, whom he paid. In 1993 his wife was the province's director of finance and his son was the chairman of the district committee responsible for finance, military, and security affairs. All of them have close ties with both the Thai Army and the Phnom Penh army. They sell the area's natural resources—fish, shrimp, timber—to Thailand for their own profit. Similar deals are concocted by others all over the country.

In the weeks before its departure in September 1993, UNTAC had almost 200 cars and trucks stolen. Most of the thefts were carried out by gangs organized by senior officials of the old regime. UNTAC named some of the officials and generals it believed to be responsible, but for months nothing was done to stop or apprehend them.

By the end of 1993 the rash of robberies had become an epidemic. The ringleaders were police and military officers from the CPP. Generals' wives were to be seen driving around town in newly painted four-wheel drive Toyotas that had belonged to UNTAC. The government was unable or unwilling to crack down on this organized crime.

By early 1994 more than 300 U.N. vehicles had been stolen. Nate Thayer reported in the *Far Eastern Economic Review* that on 12

January, as foreign aid workers gathered to protest the spate of robberies and the role of government agents in them, the police shot three robbers dead as they broke into a U.N. compound to steal cars. One of those killed was a uniformed policeman and two were the personal bodyguards of Chea Sim, the chairman of the CPP and head of the National Assembly.

That was no surprise; everyone knew that government officials and military officers were involved in every level of the banditry. One U.N. vehicle was brazenly on display at the Pursat police headquarters. The police chief had demanded $3,000 for its return to UNHCR. In February 1994 several senior officials were finally arrested and the theft of foreigners' vehicles began to taper off. But with more and more unpaid soldiers roaming the countryside, the provinces were becoming increasingly dangerous.

Cambodian society still needs to be completely overhauled. When the founders of the Khmer Rouge originally left Phnom Penh for the maquis in the 1960s, they did so because of the pervasive corruption and inequality of a country dominated then, as now, by Sihanouk. Unless the new government, and the new king, make the sustained effort necessary to generate changes in society, some of the conditions that first inspired support for that bloody revolution could once again assert themselves.

Determination by Cambodia's rulers will have to be matched by continued interest from the international community. There is a danger that the international attention that was so vital in helping Cambodia address its problems in recent years has now turned away in the belief that those problems are solved. They are not. Indeed, it should be clear from the Cambodian example that a peacekeeping mission needs follow-through and sustained commitment if, in the long run, it is to change a society. If the success of UNTAC is to be built upon, continued international interest, pressure, and assistance is vital.

The following chapters review some of the principal problem areas, foreign and domestic, that imperil the new Cambodia's relative peace and its development. After a number of specific issues—coalition politics, human rights, the role of the media, and security—a chapter on the economy touches on the viability of domestic rejuvenation. This survey is hardly meant to be exhaustive, but it makes a case for continued international support for and monitoring of a very fragile national reconciliation.

The Coalition

At the beginning of 1994 political omens in Phnom Penh were mixed. Prince Ranariddh had been promoted to First Prime Minister. He exuded energy and growing confidence. He was visible, at least in Phnom Penh, and he talked of getting the country moving, insisting that it must grow enough rice to become self-sufficient.

But some critics argued that the prince had not really articulated a sense of priority or of urgency on the principal issues facing Cambodia. Others went further and said there was a general sense of drift in the government.

Ranariddh, his co-Prime Minister Hun Sen, and other leading members of the coalition sometimes showed more interest in foreign travel or in fripperies than in setting an agenda for the country. Too often FUNCINPEC's leadership seemed more interested in cosmetic measures than in real changes. Thus, Cambodia's first beauty contest was staged in fall 1993—and the winner was crowned by Ranariddh's wife Princess Marie, with the runner-up honored by Mrs. Hun Sen. Between $2 million and $4 million were spent on boat races and fireworks for the Independence Day celebrations on 9 November 1993. Ranariddh ordered the Phnom Penh port on the river to be moved so that a park could be created. It sometimes appeared that the government was more concerned with decor than with reconstruction and that Ranariddh did not really enjoy facing the difficult decisions needed. If so, his attitude may have reflected the gridlock endemic to the coalition. His critics felt that early on he should have grasped the leadership role much more firmly. In March 1994 Ranariddh increased such concerns when he left Cambodia for a two-week stay in Aix-en-Provence, resuming his old teaching post. That seemed a strange priority for a new prime minister.

By the end of 1993 there was reasonably good cooperation amongst most ministers. (In the new government there were 17 ministries as against 30 in the provisional government.) But the Cabinet met rarely, displaying little cohesion. In early December Ranariddh called his new Minister of Information, Ieng Mouly, to ask about a proposed press conference by Hun Sen. Ieng Mouly knew nothing about it; the arrangements had been made exclusively by one of his CPP deputies, who had not bothered to inform the minister. More serious lapses occurred frequently.

In most ministries, FUNCINPEC's power diminished the further down the hierarchy one looked—it simply did not have enough people. And in the provinces FUNCINPEC made no progress until the turn of the year. The CPP had spun out talks on surrendering provincial power—which meant real power over the bulk of the people—since June. For the majority of Cambodians very little had changed in the way they were governed.

FUNCINPEC had a basic problem: lack of its own personnel. Indeed, one must acknowledge that, without its coalition partners, it would have been quite unable to function at all: the process of governing depended completely on CPP personnel in all the ministries. In the official news agency, SPK, for example, there were 600 jobs—all of them filled by CPP appointees. Much the same was true of many other government offices.

What was not clear in early 1994 was how many such people were beginning to shift their allegiances away from the CPP and towards FUNCINPEC or the BLDP.

There were two conflicting analyses. One, propagated by FUNCINPEC officials, was that FUNCINPEC was quietly burrowing into the power and strongholds of the CPP. The other was that FUNCINPEC's hold on power really was restricted only to the top, to cabinet level, and that structural power remained in the hands of the CPP. Most important of all, FUNCINPEC seemed to have made no inroads into the security services.

In November 1993 the *Phnom Penh Post*'s chief political writer, Nate Thayer, agitated senior FUNCINPEC officials with an article entitled "Who's Really In Control?" which suggested that despite the election victory of FUNCINPEC, the CPP retained an almost exclusive grip on power, and that Cambodia's traditional methods of government—intimidation, factional power bases, violence—still prevailed.

That analysis was challenged by FUNCINPEC Minister of Finance Rainsy, who said, "The CPP knows they are fighting a rear-guard action. They know the trend is not for the CPP. The trend is for democracy. The development of the country means political transparency and that is against the CPP interests." A few months later Rainsy was less confident.

Moreover, FUNCINPEC's Foreign Minister, Prince Norodom Sirivudh, could argue that he then controlled all external delegations and decided whom they should see. Rainsy had also begun to centralize all revenue collection. Provincial governments were now required, in theory, to transfer revenues to the government in Phnom Penh.

Other senior officials, some close to Sihanouk, were more pessimistic, arguing that FUNCINPEC leaders were too keen on the trappings of office, wielding little real power. But FUNCINPEC ministers argued that the CPP leaders had profited so well from the coalition with FUNCINPEC that they had little reason to undermine it. In fact, FUNCINPEC had been courting such alleged CPP "hardliners" as Sar Kheng and Chea Sim. Chea Sim, the head of the party and the principal rival to Hun Sen, had become Chairman of the National Assembly (and effective head of state in the absence of the king). He had also been awarded the precious honorific title, *Samdech*, or President—a rare privilege that was also accorded to Hun Sen in spring 1994. Some FUNCINPEC officials characterized his honors as making him *"plus royalist que le roi,"* and erasing his communist beliefs. Others felt that was overly sanguine. Thus Julio Jeldres, a former close aide to King Sihanouk and director of the Khmer Institute for Democracy, which tried to inculcate and reinforce democratic ideas in students, argued that FUNCINPEC must realize that since the election the CPP had "employed its most trusted instruments—violence and deception—to throttle the government and derail the transition to democracy. The hardliners' strategy is clearly to retain power without overthrowing the new government." He insisted that the only way in which

FUNCINPEC could hope to rebuild Cambodia was "to protect and nurture the newly acquired rights of the people."

Sar Kheng, the Minister of Interior and a Vice Prime Minister, had an unsavory past in the CPP's security services. As minister he was thought to have been involved in the CPP's officially sanctioned death squads that attacked FUNCINPEC officials at the end of 1992 and in early 1993. He later helped to block FUNCINPEC reforms. By the end of 1993 he was a crucial force in both the CPP and the coalition. The U.S. embassy had already invited him and a FUNCINPEC official to the United States. In spring 1994 he went on a well-trodden tour for those foreign leaders the U.S. hopes to captivate; designed to impress visitors with the virtues of democratic behavior, it included staying with an American family. That invitation caused understandable outrage amongst some human rights groups and others in Phnom Penh, though embassy officials deny that any protest was made to them. U.S. government officials explained that they were trying to show Sar Kheng democracy in action. The U.S. clearly recognized his continuing power. Upon his return, one of his aides said privately that the trip had indeed opened Sar Kheng's eyes to different values and political processes.

Until early 1994 FUNCINPEC had been a resistance movement rather than a political party; it had infiltrated many branches of the CPP and the SOC, but it had not established an organized base in the country. In the provinces power remained in the hands of the governors and district and local police and security apparats. Sam Rainsy acknowledged that "central authority has very little knowledge—not even to speak of control—of the provinces."

In December 1993 the distribution of provincial governorships was finally decided. The CPP kept two of the most important provinces FUNCINPEC had won in the election: Battambang and Kompong Cham. In each the CPP had a notoriously corrupt governor—in Kompong Cham it was Hun Sen's brother. Koh Kong province and its corruption also remained in the hands of the CPP. But FUNCINPEC obtained a strategic corridor of provinces linking Phnom Penh and the port of Sihanoukville. Government leaders (led by Sam Rainsy) hoped to develop it into the main commercial zone of the country.

By early 1994 corruption also threatened to infect, if not destroy, the FUNCINPEC leadership. In Phnom Penh rumors circulated that this or that senior official was accepting the standard suitcase of money or foreign stock shares, brought by Southeast Asian businessmen in exchange for government contracts. That is not surprising, considering the low formal salaries of $30–$60 a month of most ministers and officials.

Of the three principal political factions, FUNCINPEC is probably the poorest. The Khmer Rouge still have the vast resources of western Cambodia that they continue to steal and exploit. They also have business investments in both Thailand and Phnom Penh, and large accounts in Chinese banks. The CPP has expropriated large areas of real estate in Phnom Penh and other regions; party officials also continue to steal timber and other natural resources—quite apart from the thefts conducted by CPP members of the security forces.

In early 1994 all popular expectations rested with FUNCINPEC and to a lesser extent with the BLDP. It was they, not the CPP, who were expected to deliver change. The CPP could afford to sit back—nothing was expected of them. For the Khmer Rouge, time was also a resource.

And yet, Ranariddh, facing a daunting test, had failed to establish a clear sense of direction. Given the extent of Cambodia's needs in every sector of life, it was undoubtedly a hard task. But it had to be faced—as King Sihanouk frequently pointed out. Otherwise FUNCINPEC would dissipate its mandate. Indeed, by spring 1994, people complained almost as much about FUNCINPEC as they did about the CPP; the party and its leaders had already lost enormous good will.

Amongst the most urgent requirements was a policy to deal with the Khmer Rouge. But they cannot be dealt with in isolation. There is a Catch-22 problem here: the Khmer Rouge will be finally defeated only if the government succeeds, but the government cannot succeed without their defeat—or at least their isolation.

The Khmer Rouge and Thailand

The Khmer Rouge were seriously weakened by the election. But they still receive assistance from Thailand and remain a threat to the stability and integrity of the Royal Government. As the 1994 dry season began, fighting once more started between Khmer Rouge and government forces in the north and west of Cambodia.

In the last twenty-three years predictions of Khmer Rouge strength and strategies have rarely proved correct. They are currently thought to have some 10,000 troops, but even that is uncertain.

One of the most important issues is that of defection—which the new government should be doing everything to encourage. The number of Khmer Rouge who have actually defected to the new government since the election is in dispute. The government has claimed at least 3,000. But the figure has been swollen by considerable numbers of impostors. According to an investigation by the *Phnom Penh Post*, in one center for Khmer Rouge defectors, Russey Keo camp, only 37 of the 397 alleged guerrillas were genuine. The others were FUNCINPEC soldiers or poor peasants who had paid bribes to corrupt generals to gain entry into the unified army.

Most of the genuine Khmer Rouge defectors were young soldiers who had joined the Khmer Rouge during the years of Vietnamese occupation. Many of them said they wanted to return to being farmers in their native villages, but they were frightened of retribution. In December 1993 two defectors were reported to have been executed by the Khmer Rouge in Siem Reap province.

The defection program could have been given a higher priority by the government. Instead, it has been badly managed and even counterproductive. Monies are scarce. Defectors have been greeted with poor conditions, even with brutality. Reeducation has been harsh; promises have been broken. The overall effect has been to discourage further defections. Some defectors said that while conditions under Khmer Rouge leadership were tough, those in the new Royal Army were often no better. They said that there was more corruption and pay was more erratic.

By early 1994 the government was seeking to improve its defection program. The U.S. provided some material assistance, but little foreign funding has been given because Western governments are shy of anything associated with the Khmer Rouge. Thailand can offer lessons in that regard. In the early 1980s, after China withdrew its crucial support from the Thai Communist Party, government amnesties quickly eliminated the party. But that was a large-scale program, funded by the U.S., that involved expensive rural development projects. Nothing on such a scale has been proposed for Cambodia. It is needed, even if it would be much more difficult.

Since the provisional government was formed in June 1993, talks have continued intermittently between Sihanouk and Khieu Samphan, between Ranariddh and Khieu Samphan, and between other leaders of the government and the Khmer Rouge in an attempt to find a basis for reconciliation and development.

So far all talks have failed and many of the promises the Khmer Rouge made in the Paris Agreement remain unfulfilled. They have not agreed to a ceasefire. They have not implemented the substance of Phase Two of the agreement. They have not agreed to the cantonment and demobilization of their forces. They have not provided their fellow Cambodians or the international community with access to the areas under their control. Nor have they allowed Cambodians within those areas the freedom to leave.

Nonetheless, some ministers remain optimistic. At the end of 1993, Norodom Sirivudh, the Foreign Minister and Deputy Prime Minister, argued that "The Khmer Rouge tiger is now a cat. We won't kill him. By inviting him into the living room, and manicuring and shampooing him, we will tame him. Give them milk. Make them advisers. Make Khieu Samphan governor of Pailin. They must open their zones, but they can still have them."

Such offers have not to date proved attractive to the Khmer Rouge. In November, from his hospital bed in Beijing, Sihanouk offered "acceptable" Khmer Rouge officials—a term which excludes Pol Pot and his closest colleagues—positions as co-ministers, co-secretaries of state, and advisers in the coalition "in order to solve the problem of our motherland in the spirit of national reconciliation."

Sihanouk's offer was conditional on the Khmer Rouge's meeting three conditions: They had to discontinue all acts of violence and institute a ceasefire; return the 10 per cent of the country they control, including their headquarters at Pailin; and integrate their soldiers into the Royal Cambodian Army.

Before the Khmer Rouge leadership itself had had time to reject those proposals, the government in Phnom Penh itself did so. On 27 November Sihanouk wrote to Khieu Samphan to tell him that Ranariddh had declared the idea "unconstitutional." Ranariddh had made the point that under the new constitution ministers had to come from parties represented in the National Assembly.

However, on 17 December 1993, Ranariddh himself met with Samphan and proposed changing the constitution to allow Khmer Rouge participation in the government—on the condition that they surrender their autonomy. Once again the Khmer Rouge leadership refused. Instead, Samphan demanded a 15 per cent representation in ministries and senior military positions in the integrated army, with Khmer Rouge troops remaining a distinct entity. He wanted a "working group of the patriotic movement," made up of the Khmer Rouge, FUNCINPEC, and the BLDP—and excluding the CPP. Ranariddh rejected that absurd formulation and proposed a working group composed of two Khmer Rouge members and six from the government side.

In this tripartite dialogue it was not always clear whether Sihanouk was acting in concert with his government or independently. The king has a greater emotional and political interest in reconciliation of all his "children" than do some of his ministers. Ranariddh said that he had had a "father to son" talk in Beijing with Sihanouk. "The King does not meddle in royal government affairs," he said. "He talked to me just like father and son and his formula is number one." The king and senior FUNCINPEC officials share a widespread agreement (with some from the CPP) that the country simply cannot afford open-ended war with the Khmer Rouge. They argue, correctly, that in the May election the majority of the country voted for peace, not prolonged confrontation.

But the reality of the matter is that the Khmer Rouge will have little incentive to compromise so long as the Thais offer them, as they still do, an alternative to peace. A curious reversal has taken place in government attitudes in Phnom Penh. Vietnam, for so long the bête noire of FUNCINPEC and of many Cambodians, now hardly figures as a matter of official concern in Cambodia. Instead, anxiety centers on Thailand. Foreign Minister Norodom Sirivudh has labeled Thailand "Enemy Number One" and has accused it of "scandalous" behavior. In early January he demanded to know whether the Thai government supported the royal government or the Khmer Rouge. "We want a clear stand from Thailand," he said. Thailand refused to give it.

One problem is Thai commercial activity. While investment is essential, the exploitative rapacity of Thai, or Sino-Thai business-men, ably abetted by their peers in Malaysia and Singapore, threatens to destroy many Cambodian natural assets.

On the political and military side there is a continuing alliance between the Thai military and the Khmer Rouge. Within Thailand there are, in effect, two administrations: the civilian government and the military junta that controls the border with Cambodia (and the border with Burma). The civilian government of Prime Minister Chuan Leekpai has shown signs of distancing itself from the Khmer Rouge. In December 1993 a government spokesman said, "The prime minister states clearly what the policy is—no interference in the internal affairs of Cambodia—and he expects the military and other government agencies to carry out that order."

But the administration in Bangkok, even if it meant it, has lacked the means and the will to enforce its policy, and that policy has not been followed by the relevant military units that have had such a lucrative relationship with the Khmer Rouge for years.

According to U.N. estimates, the Khmer Rouge may have been earning up to $20 million a month extracting hardwood and gems from the areas they control around Pailin in western Cambodia. Thai companies associated with members of the Thai Supreme Command have invested millions of dollars in earthmoving, digging, and lifting equipment to be used inside Cambodia. At one stage some 22,000 Thais (and Burmese) were thought to be working illegally inside Cambodia. One summer 1993 U.N. report confirmed that "for the past twelve years, the Thai military have exerted a mafia-like control. . . .The border zone has been a goldmine for them."

The uncontrolled ravaging of the land is also having a serious environmental impact. The river Sangke, leading from Pailin into the Great Lake, has been heavily polluted by the erosion caused by the open cast gem mines. It is posing a serious threat to the ecological balance of the northern end of the lake, which is Cambodia's greatest source of natural wealth: fish. The lake is silting up as a result of the erosion caused by logging. If that continues, it will be an environmental and economic catastrophe for Cambodia.

Meanwhile, the Khmer Rouge and Thai military grow richer. Some Thai military leaders still refer to the Royal Cambodian Government as a mere "faction" and denigrate its achievements. In the southeast of Thailand the Thai marines appear to have established a state of their own that brooks no interference from Bangkok.

In June 1993 Winston Lord stated that Thailand had replaced China as the chief source of support for the Khmer Rouge. He said that the civilian government had made a "sincere effort" to cut off the smuggling of timber and gems from western Cambodia. "Have they completely shut it off? No. Are all the military elements in Thailand cooperating? If they were, it would be a shut off border," he said.

Those remarks elicited a furious response from some Thai officials, but they remain true in 1994. In December 1993 Thai police uncovered a 1,500–ton cache of weapons, including heavy artillery, in a warehouse close to a Khmer Rouge area on the Thai-Cambodian border. It raised suspicion that the Thai military was still arming its Khmer Rouge partners. At about the same time, the police intercepted a truck carrying five tons of weapons headed for a Khmer Rouge enclave. The Thai Army later claimed that the weapons had been "stolen" from an arms dump which was normally guarded by Special Forces. That explanation was greeted with derision in Phnom Penh. One of the men arrested with the weapons claimed that he was a Khmer Rouge soldier and that the guns were destined for Khmer Rouge headquarters at Pailin. They had been delivered some years previously by China and stockpiled in Thailand ever since.

In mid-January Thai Prime Minister Chuan paid an official visit to Cambodia in an attempt to repair relations. The visit seemed to achieve little.

January 1994 also saw a traditional "dry season offensive" against the Khmer Rouge by government forces. In early February government forces captured the Khmer Rouge northern headquarters of Anlong Veng, in the north of Siem Reap province. Foreign military analysts told the *Phnom Penh Post* that at least 200 government soldiers were killed.

Anlong Veng was the base of Ta Mok, a one-legged general who was one of the strongest and most brutal of the Khmer Rouge leaders. According to press reports he left behind his artificial limbs when he fled.

A Khmer Rouge spokesman, Mak Ben, denied that the base had fallen and said, "The war will not solve the problem. The war has lasted fifteen years. They are fighting the sixteenth dry season. The military situation will not change the balance of forces."

Three weeks later the Khmer Rouge in fact drove the government troops out of Anlong Veng. It was a humiliating and costly defeat for Phnom Penh and reflected poor morale as well as lack of equipment and supplies, especially ammunition.

On 19 March 1994, the government launched another offensive and captured the Khmer Rouge's headquarters at Pailin, close to the Thai border, and about 220 miles northwest of Phnom Penh. The intention was to capture not only the headquarters but also logging and mining equipment belonging to Thai companies. There were obvious dangers and in Beijing King Sihanouk voiced his concerns, telling visitors that he feared the Khmer Rouge were preparing a trap and that the government could suffer a major defeat.

Throughout March 1994, the government held Pailin. Perhaps more important, its troops had also captured a good deal of the mining and logging equipment installed in Khmer Rouge areas by Thai companies. That should have enabled Phnom Penh to bargain more effectively with the Thai authorities, but when Phnom Penh asked the Thais to allow the 25,000 or so refugees—mostly in fact from Khmer Rouge areas—who had fled the fighting into Thailand to return voluntarily to areas of their choice, Thailand refused. The Thai military, furious at the disruption of its profitable gem and timber trade with the Khmer Rouge, also refused UNHCR and the International Committee of the Red Cross access to the refugees. Instead, the military forced them back across the border into Khmer Rouge areas.

That led the Bangkok paper, *The Nation*, to comment, "Once again the image Thailand has presented to the world has been of conspicuously sleazy border traders enriching themselves under the administration of the military and of Cambodian refugees caught up in a murky political game." It called the forced return of the refugees "staggering in its insensitivity and shortsightedness." There was no arguing with such criticisms. Indeed, the U.N. High Commissioner for Refugees, Sadako Ogata, lodged a forceful protest with the Thai government, taking "strong exception" to Thailand's behavior.

In spring 1994 at one level it could appear that nothing had changed: fighting between Phnom Penh and the Khmer Rouge continued as it has for two and a half decades, except for the years 1975–78 when the Khmer Rouge were themselves in Phnom Penh and fighting the rest of the population. But the changes are still enormous. UNTAC and the election did inflict a historic defeat on the Khmer Rouge. Their former allies were subsequently ranged against them. They had very little international support—outside of the Thai military.

Nonetheless, the Khmer Rouge are convinced that time is on their side. There is some reason to believe that they may be planning to activate their National Union Party, which was created at the end of 1992 and which might be developed as a legitimate opposition. Since the beginning of 1994 more and more references to that party have been heard on Khmer Rouge radio.

The Khmer Rouge are also constantly trying to drive wedges between FUNCINPEC and the CPP. Mak Ben, the Khmer Rouge spokesman, made the point that "with fighting, rehabilitation and construction is out of the question. There can be no peace, no security, and no foreign investment."

However weakened the Khmer Rouge were by the election and by defections, it will be very difficult for the new army actually to defeat them by force—at least so long as they have the sanctuaries of Thailand for resupply and protection. And even an end to Thai support would not mean the demise of the Khmer Rouge.

In April 1994 Sihanouk's earlier fears were confirmed as the Khmer Rouge took back Pailin after a series of disastrous military setbacks for the government forces.

Only the success of the royal government in genuinely changing Cambodian society to the benefit of ordinary Cambodians will finally break the bizarre and vicious spell the Khmer Rouge hold over some Cambodians and over the country's political development. The Khmer Rouge are false revolutionaries. The revolution needs to come from Phnom Penh. By mid-1994 there were disturbing signs that it would not happen.

The Monarchy

Sihanouk still arches over the Cambodian polity, but his cancer has invoked for the first time a public discussion of the death of the man who has dominated Cambodian life for fifty years. Indeed, after his cancer was diagnosed, Sihanouk himself acknowledged, "My death is foreseeable."

His decline was apparent even on the streets. In 1991, when he returned to Phnom Penh, large paintings around the town depicted him as youthful, as when he had first ruled. Now the paintings have been replaced by more somber, greyhaired portraits of him and the queen. The government appears to be alerting the population to his mortality.

After his brief visit to Phnom Penh to be crowned and to ratify the constitution in September 1993, the king began treatment for cancer in the private wing of a hospital in Beijing. Queen Monique and a number of courtiers remained with him. He had six rounds of chemotherapy in Beijing.

At the end of 1993 it was reported that the cancer had infected his bone marrow, but that it was expected to go into remission. He was still well enough to dispatch dozens of daily letters and faxes from his bed. In the early months after his coronation, Sihanouk acted beneficently, guiding rather than issuing orders from afar. But as his concern about the lack of direction and drive in the government grew, so, apparently, did his own frustration with lack of formal power.

Some diplomats argued that it was helpful that he was out of town. Ranariddh and Hun Sen would have to try and reach decisions on their own, yet, in the event of disagreement, the king could still serve as the court of last resort and arbitrate between the factions. His own overriding personal ambition was still to effect a national reconciliation of all factions, including the Khmer Rouge. As for the issue of succession, a number of scenarios are possible, but their nature and outcome depend on when he dies.

The Cambodian kingship has traditionally been elective rather than hereditary. Article 14 of the new constitution restricts the choice. It states that the monarch must be "a member of the Khmer Royal Family, aged at least 30 years, coming from the blood line of the King Ang Duong, Norodom or Sisowath."

The actual choice has to be made by the Royal Council of the Throne within seven days of the death or abdication of the monarch. The committee is presided over by Chea Sim, Chairman of the Assembly; the two prime ministers, Ranariddh and Hun Sen; the vice presidents of the Assembly; and two supreme monks of both principal Buddhist orders in Cambodia.

Many foreigners assume that Ranariddh would be the automatic choice to succeed Sihanouk and that his father has in effect already endorsed him. In early December 1993 Sihanouk told the *Phnom Penh Post* that Ranariddh could continue to work as a political leader until he was elected king. "He will then have to cease directing a political party and governing the country, and will be a King who will reign but will not rule."

But it would be hard for Ranariddh to abandon his political commitments and place himself above the fray. Moreover, he has publicly declared his intention to stay in politics.

There are alternatives, and some of their causes might well be pushed by different factions or parts of the court.

In terms of strict lineage, Prince Chakrapong, Ranariddh's hated half-brother, has a better claim than Ranariddh himself. He and his older brother, Prince Yuvaneath, are the only surviving offspring of Sihanouk and a royal mother. The other seven living children were born to non-royal mothers. (Six other fully royal children died, or were murdered by the Khmer Rouge.) In early 1994 Yuvaneath returned to Phnom Penh, apparently to establish his claim.

Queen Monique, whose relations with Ranariddh are not close, is thought to favor the succession of her own eldest son, Prince Sihamoni. This prince, now 30 years old, has never shown much interest in politics. He is a ballet dancer in Paris and currently serves as Cambodia's ambassador to the United Nations Educational, Scientific and Cultural Organization (UNESCO). He has starred in several of his father's films.

Sihamoni's apolitical life might make him acceptable to all factions. The king's former counselor and confidante, Julio Jeldres, told the *Phnom Penh Post* that he would be ideal: "He is a complete artist only interested in music. . . . Thus he would make a great patron of the arts and ancient Khmer culture and tradition." Sihanouk himself has said that Sihamoni is his second choice, after Ranariddh. But it is not clear that the prince would wish to exchange the freedoms of Paris for the intrigues of the court in Phnom Penh.

Some FUNCINPEC officials would like to see Prince Norodom Sirivudh, present Foreign Minister, Deputy Prime Minister, and half-brother of the king, take on the monarchy. His chances are slim. Sirivudh himself has suggested that Cambodia should recreate the notion of a Royal *house* and bring back the Sisowath branch of the family, which the French had sidelined in 1941, as the constitution allows.

There are two elderly Sisowath princes living in exile, one in the United States and one in France. Their chances of succession are not thought to be very strong, but it is the Royal Throne Council that has to decide the issue immediately following the death of the king. Another possibility being discussed is to leave the throne vacant for a while: this option might avoid some of the worst factional fighting over the succession. A regent could be appointed.

All in all, the most likely successor is Ranariddh. The question is when. By the end of March 1994 King Sihanouk's health appeared to be improving again; he left hospital in Beijing and his spokesman said that he would soon return to Cambodia. The king seemed to visitors to be both fit and in fine form. He said that his Chinese doctors had eliminated the cancer from most of his body, but that about 0.5 per cent remained in his bone marrow. If that is correct,

then he should live many years yet. In April 1994 the king returned
to Phnom Penh, promising to stay for at least two months, but he
left again on 18 May.

The paradox is this: At one level Sihanouk is responsible for having
kept Cambodian politics immature. Even after UNTAC Phnom Penh
still functions more as a court that revolves around its king than as
a developed political system. But that being so, the focal point of the
court is desperately needed.

For Cambodia's stability in its difficult transition, the longer the
king is able to function as a stable head of state and mediator, the
better. But the king needs also to push the coalition to meet its
responsibilities and to fulfill the promises made to the people in
the election. Above all, he needs to encourage the development of
democratic institutions. In April and May he gave conflicting signals
of his desire and ability to do this.

What is certain is that whoever succeeds Sihanouk will not be
able to command the same loyalty and attention that Sihanouk
enjoys. On his death, Cambodian politics are likely to become more
unsettled still—unless he has managed to encourage the institutions
of modern government to progress along the lines that UNTAC and
the constitution have laid out.

Parliament

The National Assembly is, so far, a disappointment. When
the Constituent Assembly ratified the constitution in September
1993, it automatically became the National Assembly. It has not
been exercising its full powers. It was intended to have three sessions
of three months per year and should have been in continuous session
from the adoption of the constitution until the end of 1993. In fact
it met only three times in plenary session during that period. In those
sessions it adopted internal rules of procedure and elected its own
leadership and the members of nine parliamentary commissions that
were to correspond to the eighteen ministries. They included commissions on foreign relations, economics, finance and banking, human

rights, education, children's and women's issues, posts and communications, trade, and transportation.

In all, 68 of the 120 members of the parliament were placed on the commissions—virtually everyone who was not already part of the government itself.

Under the constitution the commissions are supposed to initiate legislation. But it was not certain that they could or would. They lacked all the appurtenances of most parliaments: collective experience, research services for bill drafting, a library, and legal expertise.

Nevertheless, at the end of 1993 several acts of legislation were drafted, including an investment law and immigration and citizenship laws. The immigration and citizenship bill was to establish criteria for who could stay, live, and work in Cambodia, and set conditions for citizenship and border control. The definition of "citizenship" will be contentious—and crucial. But it should help deflect Khmer Rouge claims of excessive favors being done to Vietnamese immigrants, while protecting their rights as residents. By the end of May 1994, it still had not been put to the Assembly.

The Assembly's first, controversial meeting was the closed plenary session in which members debated their own remuneration. Astonishingly, they wanted to vote themselves salaries and perks worth more than $2,000 a month—in a country where the mean income is $200 a year. Both Hun Sen and Sam Rainsy argued that such compensation was too high, that the country could not afford it, and that civil servants and police would not tolerate it. Eventually, deputies settled on $650 a month, plus perks worth about another $1,000. It was still a fantastic reward, considering that ministers were being paid only about $40 a month and civil servants less.

Some Assembly members justified the high salaries as a bulwark against corruption. Furthermore, some forty deputies were expatriates who had returned from Europe, the United States, or Australia and who had responsibilities abroad that they could not possibly fulfill on the average official Phnom Penh salary. It is also worth remembering that it is very hard for parliaments in Southeast Asia to establish their independence. Nonetheless, the award generated a great deal of resentment in Phnom Penh.

By early 1994 some members of all three parties were emerging
as activists, but it was too early to tell how much independence
they would develop. Under the policy of "national reconciliation,"
no real opposition had emerged in the Assembly. Indeed, the concept
of a "loyal Opposition" was, understandably, still remote to most
Cambodians. Instead, reconciliation became the rationalization for
all compromise.

The spirit of reconciliation was sometimes taken to extremes—as
in early December 1993 when two CPP members were told by their
party to resign so Prince Chakrapong and Sin Song, the principal
architects of the June 1993 secession, could reenter parliament. The
murderous, destructive behavior of those men might have been
expected to disqualify them from any positions of responsibility
forever. Their proposed return to parliament did not bode well for
the integrity and purpose of the coalition.

Nonetheless, in its most constructive act, on 28 December 1993
the Assembly unanimously adopted a budget and new financial laws
that should allow the government to seize control of the nation's
corrupt and confused financial structures. The new laws should,
with luck, judgment, and political perseverance, create the financial
structures needed to help the country pull itself out of its economic
abyss. "This is a revolution—people do not realize I think how far
reaching it is," Sam Rainsy told the *Phnom Penh Post*. "With these
new laws we can fight dictatorship. It is a silent revolution that will
bring Cambodia back to modernity from the dark ages."

That was the view of international financial institutions also. But
both they and Rainsy underestimated the opposition to any such
changes. In the months that followed, his efforts to attack the institutionalized corruption and to centralize revenue collection engendered
fierce opposition from business interests and lost him a great deal of
support within the government itself. Indeed, the lack of support
for institutionalizing change has become a matter of great concern.
For example, by early June 1994, the government had still not
enacted an investment law or a property law; problems of owner-
ship often become critical. There is no formal or legal way to settle

the increasing number of land disputes, as people return from abroad to claim property and developers attempt to force people to move from their homes. In a society where corruption and violence still hold sway, such official dilatoriness is dangerous and will engender great resentment.

Human Rights and the Judicial System

Cambodians have always been abused by authority. In the 1950s and 1960s, Sihanouk's rule was arbitrary and quixotic and often harsh to those he considered his opponents. There was no independent judiciary.

Between April 1975 and December 1978, the Khmer Rouge destroyed what remained of the legal system and the basic institutions of a civil society. The authoritarian communist regime that the Vietnamese established in January 1979 was benign only by Khmer Rouge standards.

When UNTAC arrived an independent judiciary still did not exist; all judges were subject to the Communist Party. Large numbers of political prisoners were still held without trial or due process of law. Arbitrary arrest and detention, summary execution, excessive and unchecked use of military and police force, and denial of freedom of association were all standard practices that Amnesty International, Asia Watch, and other human rights organizations frequently condemned. Human rights in the zones run by the KPNLF, FUNCINPEC, and the Khmer Rouge were, to varying degrees, ignored or abused.

The Paris Agreement's mandate on human rights was unprecedented. It specifically created an UNTAC Human Rights Component and charged UNTAC with "fostering an environment in which respect of human rights shall be ensured." It was to promote education, to oversee human rights, to investigate abuses "and, where appropriate, take corrective action." The nature of that action was not defined. UNTAC was to spread the idea of human rights in a country where no such rights had ever been acknowledged, let alone implemented. That did not entail rebuilding a damaged institution, but creating an entirely new system—in eighteen months.

In the pre-election atmosphere of widespread intimidation and violence, the task of the Human Rights Component was formidable indeed. Not one of the Cambodian factions was willing to investigate, arrest, or prosecute people suspected of involvement in political violence. Moreover, the Component lacked adequate assistance from the rest of UNTAC; it was denied sufficient staff or logistical support to fulfill its intended role as a protagonist.

In early 1993 UNTAC, at the Component's initiative, created an Office of Special Prosecutor to prosecute serious violations of human rights. But the office languished as Akashi, Sanderson, and other UNTAC officials began to fear that prosecutorial zeal might destroy the entire mission's fragile links with the Phnom Penh regime, and in the face of continuing refusal by the parties, especially the CPP, to cooperate in prosecuting offenders.

Despite its disadvantage, UNTAC's Human Rights Component made considerable achievements. Perhaps most important, it released an extraordinary, pent-up demand for basic rights amongst ordinary Cambodians. The Component's work reflected the Cambodians' deep desire to break with the brutality of their past.

For the first time ever in Cambodia, several local human rights groups sprang up under UNTAC's protection. Boasting more than 250,000 members, the most significant were ADHOC, LICADHO, Cambodian Human Rights Association, Outreach, Vigilance, Ponleu Khmer, Ligue Cambodgienne des Droits de l'Homme et du Citoyen, and the development-oriented Khemara. Many of their members worked bravely, particularly in the provinces, where they received only limited protection from UNTAC's provincial human rights officers, who had neither the authority nor the means to protect them.

The Paris Agreement included a long-term commitment to human rights. Article 17 called on the United Nations Commission on Human Rights in Geneva to continue monitoring the human rights situation in post-UNTAC Cambodia, "including, if necessary, by the appointment of a Special Rapporteur who would report his findings annually to the Commission and to the General Assembly."

However, at the February 1993 meeting of the U.N. Commission, the ASEAN countries led an assault on the proposed appointment of a Special Rapporteur. The Foreign Minister of Indonesia, Ali Alatas, who had played an important part in formulating the Paris Agreement, informed UNTAC human rights officials that this and other clauses in the agreement were no longer relevant. That new orthodoxy among Asian countries is intended to counter the influence of the international human rights lobby.

As a result of pressure from ASEAN and China, the Human Rights Commission agreed to water down the new office to one of a Special Representative, with powers confined to education and training. Although the Geneva meeting agreed to establish—for the first time anywhere—an operational presence in Cambodia, the ASEAN-China bloc reduced its monitoring role.

After UNTAC disbanded, the new office took too long to establish. The first choice of special representative, a West African judge, demanded so much in terms of free first-class air travel and other perks that he was eventually discarded. Instead, an Australian judge, Michael Kirby, was selected. But by June 1994 the Geneva-based Human Rights Commission still had not appointed a director of the office. There were good staff already in place, but they had almost no support in terms of equipment or personnel. In December the office was still without telephones or fax machines and the salaries of the staff were not assured. By May 1994 the equipment was in place, but the office was still funded only on a monthly basis.

Nonetheless, there are grounds for optimism. On 11 December 1993, Cambodia formally celebrated International Human Rights Day for the first time. It was an extraordinary occasion, considering recent history. Set up in the foyer of the Tonle Bassac meeting hall on the river were the stalls of dozens of different human rights groups. One man said, "Just think that a year ago the police were beating the hell out of us all over the country."

After the departure of UNTAC there was much less information on human rights violations in the provinces. But several of the Cambodian groups now have representatives and offices in different parts of the country and none have brought tales of widespread problems. There has been no sign that the CPP was attempting to turn back the clock.

The two largest and most active human rights groups by mid-1994 were ADHOC and LICADHO. Like many such groups in other parts of the world, they have organizational problems and are dominated by personalities. But they are here to stay. They are protected, albeit imperfectly, by the new constitution, which should act as a benchmark and a didactic instrument of what a "modern" Cambodia should be like. Most important, the constitution sets up a new judicial system.

The new system is intended to have two components. First is the Supreme Council of Judges, which is primarily an administrative body and is appointed by the king. It should include all judges, prosecutors, and other members of the legal establishment (when they exist).

Second is the Constitutional Council, a constitutional review board that examines the constitutionality of laws. Any law can be brought for review by the prime minister, by Assembly members, by ministers, or by the king. The Constitutional Council has nine members, intended to be "dignitaries" and not members of the Assembly. Three of them are appointed by the president of the Assembly, three by the king, and three by the Supreme Council of Judges. Thus, in effect, the king appoints six of its nine members. But by June 1994 neither of these bodies had been formed.

At a lower level, the judicial system is supposed to consist of judges, prosecutors, defenders, and the police. By mid-1994 most of those who existed needed training or, in the case of police, retraining.

After UNTAC's departure the prisons in Phnom Penh deteriorated once again. Conditions in the T3 prison and the "P.J." (Police Judiciare) prison were execrable; many of those incarcerated have not even been brought to cursory trial. Prisoners are once more being shackled. On the other hand, conditions at the Prey Sar prison, some 15 miles outside Phnom Penh, are reasonable. Prisons are now under both the Ministry of the Interior and the Ministry of Justice, whose Minister, Chem Sguon, has demonstrated some willingness to implement reforms.

Human rights and judicial training programs are urgently needed. Some are already being conducted by the Cambodian Human Rights Task Force, a coalition of Human Rights groups from the Philippines,

Sri Lanka, Thailand, Indonesia, and Pakistan that works with some of the strongest human rights groups in Cambodia. The project is financed by the International Human Rights Law Group in Washington, D.C. The Task Force has started programs in five areas: legal problems, human rights education, monitoring and protection, community development, and organizational development.

At the same time, the European Community had planned to provide funding to establish a provincial network of Cambodian Human Rights Officers under the U.N. The EC planned also to help fund Cambodian human rights nongovernmental associations (NGOs), the Human Rights Task Force, and the Human Rights Committee Commission of the National Assembly. By June 1994 the EC contribution was still only a promise.

In January 1994 the International Human Rights Law Group began a program to train public defenders. That scheme is funded by the U.S. Agency for International Development through the Asia Foundation. The International Court of Justice initiated a program to train judges, but in early 1994 the money, from Japan, was still held up. There is as yet no program for the training of prosecutors. And perhaps most important, there is no real attempt as yet to retrain the police to respect law and human rights. Under Hun Sen, judges, prosecutors, and police all worked hand in hand; to a large extent, they still do.

By early 1994 there were signs that some judges were trying to make independent judgments—but their rulings have often (but not always) been ignored. The real problem lay in the police, who were still answerable only to the hardline former communists who still ran the Ministry of the Interior and National Security. Judges admitted privately that they, like everyone else, were terrified of the police.

A further problem in the development of a better judicial system is the tension between France and the Anglo-Saxon donors. Indeed, that tension forms a subtext to the entire debate over development and reform in Cambodia. Although French officials in Phnom Penh had opposed much of the work of UNTAC's Human Rights Component, they were interested in the judicial system. By the end of 1993 they had persuaded the Minister of Justice, Chem Sguon, (himself a gradu-ate of French college) to institute the French legal system in the Law School. That meant a four-year course for lawyers with almost the entire first year being devoted to the study of French. To some non-French speakers that seemed an indulgence Cambodia could ill afford. In Southeast Asia the lingua franca is English and most countries have a legal code closer to the Anglo-Saxon common law than to the Napoleonic Code.

The UNTAC period was a golden age for human rights in Cambodia. If the coalition does not vigorously defend human rights and the judicial process, it stands little chance of building a stable, civil society. Vigilant outside support from the relevant international organi-zations and NGOs can only help to consolidate the gains of the UNTAC era.

Human Rights groups are all the more essential in Cambodia now because they represent, in effect, the only opposition to the new coalition government. The other sector that can monitor the coalition is an independent media.

The Media

"Everyone has the right to freedom of opinion and expression; this right includes the freedom to hold opinions without inter-ference and to seek, receive and impart information and ideas through any media and regardless of frontiers."
—Article 19 of the Universal Declaration of Human Rights.

The idea of an independent press was never strong in Cambo-dia. One 1957 study commented, "The art of public criticism is not highly developed in Cambodia, and extremes of adverse criticism of the government are met with drastic punishment." By the mid-1960s, as many as thirteen dailies, two weeklies, three monthlies, a Sunday supplement, a daily mimeographed press summary, and a daily journal of criticism existed in Cambodia. But they rarely had more than one opinion: that of the Chief of State, Prince Norodom

Sihanouk. Although the press was not formally censored, its content rarely strayed from that of the government press summaries.

When General Lon Nol seized power in March 1970, he at once imposed official censorship on all media (foreign as well as domestic). Though the measure was lifted in August 1970, the government continued its tight control. In June 1972 the government closed down four dailies for such alleged offenses as "disseminating false news, disrupting public order [and] damaging the unity of the Khmer people and insulting the government."

Nothing, of course, compared to the destruction of the press and restriction on freedom of thought and expression under the Khmer Rouge. A great many journalists died between 1975 and 1978 under a regime that prohibited the existence of all media except the state-controlled radio. In the early 1980s seven news organizations were created—four newspapers and a state news agency, radio, and television service—but all were controlled by the Communist Party or government.

The UNTAC period witnessed Cambodia's first flourishing of the free exchange of ideas—at least in Phnom Penh. Newspaper publishing surged. In addition to bulletins and newspapers put out by political parties, such as FUNCINPEC's *Neak Chea Niym* (*The Nationalist*) and *Realities Cambodgiennes* (*Cambodian Reality*), came a score of publications produced by independent editors operating with tremendous drive and enthusiasm but little hard cash other than what they could borrow from friends. Unlike the party bulletins, most of which became defunct, the number of independent journals grew after the election, though publication schedules for many are somewhat erratic, depending as they do on the financial circumstances of the editors.

Conditions at indigenous organizations are primitive. Most lack power, telephones, and transport. Stories are written in longhand. Printing houses are short of paper and ink as well as efficient, modern presses; darkrooms lack chemicals, equipment, and paper. According to a UNESCO report, Cambodia also lacks an effective distribution network to get papers to the provinces, a common advertising selling and billing agency to boost the income of the independent editors so they can produce more regularly, and a provincial news network.

In addition to indigenous newspapers, a number of foreign-owned publications now grace the newsstands, themselves a new phenomenon. The most successful of those, and the one generally acknowledged to have the highest circulation in Cambodia, is *Rasmei Kampuchea* (*Light of Cambodia*), owned by a Thai company and printed in Thailand, but with one of Cambodia's most experienced and skillful journalists as its Khmer editor-in-chief. A Malaysian concern publishes the *Cambodia Times*, both in English and Khmer, which ran a pro-SOC line until the results of the election were known, when it immediately became pro-coalition.

French interests are associated with *Le Mekong*, which serves all of Indochina, and *La Voix du Cambodge*; American and Japanese interests are served by the *Cambodia Daily*, which is published in English, Japanese, and Khmer. Sino-Khmer interests are about to publish a commercial bulletin in Chinese, and other Chinese concerns are considering the possibility of Chinese editions in Cambodia. The fortnightly *Phnom Penh Post*, owned by an American family and printed in Thailand, is the most authoritative foreign-language paper in the country.

UNTAC sowed the seeds for a free press. It compelled the government to provide the opposition parties with radio and television time. It insisted that the SOC allow FUNCINPEC to start a radio and television station. Most important, it established Radio UNTAC, which played a vital role in educating the population about the election. Together with other branches of UNTAC's Information-Education Division and of the Electoral Component, Radio UNTAC convinced people that their vote really would be secret, a considerable achievement in a country where such a concept was previously unknown.

Radio UNTAC ceased broadcasting in September 1993 before it and its trained Cambodian staff could be taken over by a commercial enterprise, and now Cambodia once again lacks a broadcast antidote to the propaganda of the government. The Cambodian government has been given the equipment used by Radio UNTAC but lacks the funds and personnel to operate it. One suggestion being considered is to turn the whole facility into an educational radio station.

No commercial radio exists that will broadcast nonpartisan information to Cambodians. The new Ministry of Information has, however, requested international assistance from UNESCO and other organizations to develop the state radio and television stations into independent entities along the lines of the BBC. The Minister for Foreign Affairs, Prince Norodom Sirivudh, has been reported as saying publicly that "those who work for the Ministry of Information must be neutral and must not think the national radio or the television stations belong to either the Cambodian People's Party or FUNCINPEC or any other party. They belong to the nation and the people and the Government treats them as its watchdogs."

The new Minister of Information, Ieng Mouly, a senior member of the minority BLDP, promised at his induction ceremony that his ministry would remain neutral and has encouraged the formation of an independent professional association for journalists. At a seminar on journalistic ethics funded by UNESCO and AIDAB, the aid agency of the Australian government, he said that the ministry would not and did not have the power to close down newspapers and that its function was to advise rather than to censor.

Later, when Ieng Mouly was quoted as saying that journalists might be arrested if they criticized the king, Sihanouk himself sent a message from Beijing urging that criticisms of him be allowed. Nonetheless, issues of one paper, *Sacol*, were seized after it criticized the king.

The Australian Journalists' Association has been running journalism courses in Phnom Penh since 1991. Those are now supported by AIDAB and UNESCO; early in 1994 they will publish a Khmer training manual. Since 1992 the cultural section of the French Embassy has supported a journalism training program in French for fourth- and fifth-year students of French at the University of Phnom Penh. France also has an extensive bilateral program of assistance to the state radio and television stations.

UNESCO was nominated in 1992 as the lead agency to coordinate media training and development in Cambodia, often in tandem with Danida, the aid agency of the Danish government. In October 1993 Danida agreed to provide US$375,000 towards the establishment of the Cambodia Communication Institute, with France contributing a further US$200,000. The project is to be implemented by UNESCO, which is involved in discussions with a number of other possible donors. The first formal classes through the institute are scheduled to commence at the start of the next academic year in Cambodia, September 1994, though UNESCO has a comprehensive training program of courses scheduled from January 1994 in association with both AIDAB and Danida.

Nonetheless, the threat of censorship has returned. Articles on corruption and government incompetence have irritated senior ministers. The Ministry of Information has asked newspapers not to publish photographs of either scantily clad women or dead bodies. The latter might discourage foreign investment, they say. Ministry officials have also begun to warn newspapers not to publish material that portrays the country in a negative light.

More ominously there has been talk of resurrecting a harsh press law passed quickly by the SOC in April 1992 and then declared void under pressure from UNTAC. The law authorized fines of 1 million riel for publishing "ill-intentioned" or "destructive" criticism, forced newspapers to publish on the front page any denials or corrections issued by a ministry, and allowed only Cambodian citizens to publish a paper. The last restriction would affect at least seven publications in Phnom Penh and would seriously compromise the freedom of the press in Cambodia.

On that, as on other issues, there were differences of view at the top. In March 1994 Ieng Mouly described the draft of the new press law then being considered by the Council of Ministers as "the most liberal in the world." But his CPP deputy, Khieu Kannarith, stated by contrast that the government would soon have sweeping powers to close down newspapers. Once again, King Sihanouk took the part of liberalism and sent a message from Beijing, saying, "I don't think we need to draft regulations or laws for Khmer and foreign journalists."

In the hope of preempting draconian legislation, Cambodian journalists began to develop their own indigenous professional organization and asked for further assistance from the Australian Journalists Association to draw up a code of ethics. They have set up preliminary links with journalist organizations in Thailand and Malaysia, as well as with the International Federation of Journalists.

As of the end of May 1994, the controversial, restrictive draft law had been withdrawn for further review. Information Minister Ieng Mouly said that he hoped to present a more liberal draft that conformed to international covenants and guaranteed press freedom. His problem was that he faced fierce opposition not only at the top of the CPP but also at the top of FUNCINPEC. There were few ministers who supported the idea of a free press. The threat to an independent media was considerable—and in June 1994 the situation of all journalists became more perilous after the murder of the editor-in-chief of the newspaper *Intervention*. Yet without a free media, there will not be a free, well-governed Cambodia.

CHAPTER 3

The Security Dilemma

Sovereignty. Revitalization and reform of the army, police, and justice ministry are prerequisites to the creation of a functional civil society. Cambodia also needs to regain control over its own territory, which is constantly being undermined from both within and without.

Cambodia has borders with Thailand, Laos, and Vietnam that are 600, 404, and 930 kilometers long, respectively. The fourth border is to the South China Sea. None are secure.

In Cambodia borders have always been a bandits' and rebels' wonderland, as the government's writ has faded the further it stretched from Phnom Penh. Over decades, uncontrollable borders have contributed significantly to the failure of the state. In the 1950s and 1960s the border with Thailand was haven to right-wing opponents of Prince Sihanouk. In the 1960s and 1970s, the borders with Vietnam and Laos were increasingly usurped by the communists. Today, the borders illustrate the corruption eating at every level of Cambodian society.

One 1993 UNTAC paper argued that "Phnom Penh might as usefully be located on Mars—its policies and dictates have no effect in the border marches." That is not entirely true: in some border areas corruption has been directly controlled by ministers in Phnom Penh.

People move back and forth across the Cambodia-Vietnam border constantly and uncontrollably. The Khmer Rouge allegation that there are still 2 million Vietnamese troops and settlers in the country is grossly exaggerated, but there are probably between 500,000 and 1 million settlers. In spring 1993, after the Khmer Rouge massacred scores of Vietnamese, most of them on the Great Lake or Tonle

Sap, tens of thousands fled to Vietnam. By spring 1994 several thousand displaced people—mostly women, children, and the elderly—remained in wretched conditions on the river frontier, wanted by neither government.

People do not move alone; smuggling across all borders is vast. All factions, not just the Khmer Rouge, have been guilty of stealing Cambodia's resources. It has been happening in the "liberated" zones of western Cambodia under control of the noncommunist factions and along the Lao and Vietnamese borders under the control of the Phnom Penh authorities.

The final report of one U.N. border control officer, Alick Longhurst, stationed at Poipet, one of the main crossings between Thailand and Cambodia, stated that the Cambodian police and military there "are engaged in smuggling, extortion and other illegal activities which subvert or completely deny the exercise of the border control function."

The Hun Sen regime indulged in comparable timber sales through Vietnam. Some estimates assumed that at least 40 per cent of all Cambodian-Vietnamese trade was illegal under the Hun Sen regime. Along the Lao border illegal trading of drugs and timber has also been extensive. Lao workers and soldiers in the northeastern provinces of Cambodia have engaged in logging, blatantly ignoring the ban, with the connivance of officers of the Phnom Penh armed forces. Trucks laden with timber stream into Laos.

The massive thefts taking place at Cambodia-Thai bordercross #8 (Poipet) in 1993 illustrated the extent of the problem. One CPP-appointed colonel "owned" nearly all of the major illegal crossing points on that part of the border with Thailand controlled by Phnom Penh. He made most of his income ($8,000–$12,000 a month) from the import of stolen cars from Thailand and the illegal export of rice from Cambodia, a practice banned by the Supreme National Council in an attempt to keep rice prices in Cambodia low.

UNTAC was slow to address the problems of the border. In early 1993 the U.N. established a Border Control Unit to monitor the official crossing points. UNTAC's presence had some impact. Its border control officers found, insofar as one can generalize, that customs officers were more diligent than the police. The border officers attempted to set an example for Cambodian officials who, in many cases, began to do their jobs more conscientiously. By early June the unit had trained 150 Cambodian officials from the SOC, the KPNLF, and the Sihanoukists. After the election, their work was complicated by the attempted removal of assets from Cambodia by members of the former regime. Illegal logging and the drug trade along the Lao border increased.

After the Border Control Unit was disbanded, Cambodia still lacked an efficient and honest customs and excise service. Finance Minister Sam Rainsy acted to curb the worst excesses of theft at Pochentong airport and at Sihanoukville and to ensure that customs revenues come to the Ministry of Finance. But it was only a start.

Matters were further complicated by a dispute between the Ministry of Foreign Affairs and the Ministry of National Security over customs oversight. None of the various offices at the border had a distinct chain of command or function. Immigration, police, military, and customs officers were all intermingled and involved in corruption or intimidation.

An efficient and honest customs and excise service is essential to any new administration. But the new government does not have the expertise or the manpower. It could follow the example of Indonesia, where customs revenue collection and inspection was turned over to a private body—the Swiss-based Société Générale de Surveillance. That enterprise has run Indonesian customs efficiently for many years.

One of the serious problems behind Vietnamese and Thai border incursions is the prolonged disagreement over where Cambodia's borders actually are. No boundary commission has undertaken the extremely contentious and difficult task of determining their location. Sihanouk wishes to restore the borders delineated in "the 1954 map"—but the U.N. has found that these do not exist. Sihanouk has also demanded that Hanoi and Bangkok return territory they have annexed.

In a series of communiqués in 1993, Sihanouk described a Vietnam that "used to take the kings of Cambodia and put them in cages and throw them in the ocean." Thailand and Vietnam have always taken advantage of Cambodia, abusing its sovereignty and demanding extraterritorial rights. Cambodia will never be able to deal with its neighbors as an equal until its frontiers are secure—first in principle, then in practice. As of now there is no sign of concessions by, or even negotiations with, either neighbor.

The Armed Forces. The merger of the three armies—of the People's Party, the Sihanoukists, and the Khmer People's National Liberation Front—took place on paper, but continued infighting, dry payrolls, and low morale undermined cohesion.

Worst of all, the merger did not reduce the overall size of the armed forces. The national payrolls are now closer to 160,000 than to the figure of 128,000 established by UNTAC's Operation Paymaster. By April 1994 there were 2,000 generals and 10,000 colonels in the army. It was nothing short of grotesque.

There are many reasons for that. The first is fear of demobilization and its social consequences in a society where there is still no alternative employment. Second, there is no peace with the Khmer Rouge. Third, there are fears that reduction might deter Khmer Rouge defections— because their soldiers had been promised positions in the united army if they came across.

Perhaps even more serious for social stability, the payments system established by Operation Paymaster has broken down. Although the Ministry of Finance succeeded in raising revenues, there was a liquidity crisis in the country and by mid-March 1994 payrolls were running weeks, and in some places months, behind.

The army is still poorly equipped, principally with only old Soviet and Chinese weapons. Apart from five M16 helicopters, it has no aviation. The navy consists of four or five serviceable Stenka patrol boats. The medical corps is poorly trained and has almost no equipment.

By the beginning of 1994, the Cambodian government had not provided donors or potential donors with a coordinated list of priorities and needs. Without some significant external support it will be difficult to maintain even the low level of effectiveness of the forces. Malaysia had given some assistance, and there were reports that Sihanouk's friend Kim Il Sung would provide some equipment. France's efforts were not altogether successful.

The French government signed an agreement on military cooperation on 6 July 1993; subsequently, a delegation under the Inspector-
General of the French Armed Forces, Admiral Pierre Calmon, spent
two weeks in Cambodia. He said that Cambodia clearly needed
assistance in every field, especially training. France wanted to identify
the best way forward and "follow it with others." He said that French
priorities were to the national army and regional law enforcement.
France would not involve itself in the Cambodian navy or the
(nonexistent) air force. The French wanted to help create a new
gendarmerie based on the French model, which, they hoped, would
be independent of CPP controls.

A French military mission was established in Phnom Penh in
October 1993; it was followed by a team sent to train the gendarmerie. But there were problems as to whether the gendarmerie should
work under the Ministry of Interior or Defense. As in France, the
gendarmerie was to be a rural force separate from the police. The
French hoped that it would help to counterbalance the police forces
dominated by the CPP. For that very reason, the CPP refused to allow
its creation.

French military advisers reckoned that the ideal size of the army
would be about 15,000 in all. Up to 50,000 was thought tolerable.
Anything larger would cripple the economy. Political and military
reality suggested it would be years before such reductions were
achieved. The French did provide some training, and they provided
two helicopters for the government's use.

At the beginning of 1994, very little other military aid was in
sight. Thailand agreed to provide 10,000 uniforms to the Cambodian
army and Thai officials stated they would await discussions between
the new government and the Khmer Rouge before making further
commitments. Australia was helping principally with military communications, enabling the General Staff to communicate for the
first time in years with regional military headquarters. Australia was
also assisting with training naval maintenance teams. It was helping
with mine clearance and military English-language training, and its
military had handed over their camp near the airport, complete
with generators and medical facilities, to the Cambodian air force.

Canada rejected a Cambodian request that its UNTAC contingent leave behind materiel with the exception of demining equipment. Canada was not prepared to become involved in any aid to the Cambodian armed forces. Ranariddh had asked Indonesia to provide new uniforms and to leave behind the ammunition brought by their UNTAC battalion. The Indonesian government refused to donate the ammunition, but they did agree to provide enough material to clothe three divisions—about 5,000 men. The Indonesian battalion also left vehicles, motorcycles, generators, and water purification equipment.

The United States had few plans for military assistance to Cambodia in 1994—partly on grounds of cost but largely "on grounds of history." The Cambodian government asked the U.S. to help convert Cambodian battalions into construction corps. Washington agreed to provide the extraordinary sum of $90,000 under the International Military Education and Training Program, which would provide training to half a dozen Cambodian officers. At the end of May the United States, together with Australia, France, and Malaysia, was "seriously considering" the government's request for "lethal aid." The feeling appeared to be that training and reform of the armed forces should precede the supply of weapons.

CHAPTER 4

The Need for Rehabilitation and Assistance

Cambodia has barely begun the difficult task of economic renewal. This chapter touches briefly on some of its principal economic problems.

Basic situation. The new government is essentially broke. The Soviet Union funded most expenditures in the 1980s but with the end of Soviet support in 1990, the State of Cambodia's budget went into free-fall. Revenues collapsed, expenditure was cut, and corruption began to strangle everything. The 1991 budget showed a huge financing gap, and by 1992 more than 60 per cent of total expenditures were unfunded. The state covered half the gap by printing money in Russia and flying it in—a process that produced three-figure inflation. Government officials sold off state assets as quickly as they could at distress prices, partly for personal gain and partly for current consumption. The pay of civil servants and soldiers became erratic and increasingly destroyed by inflation.

Throughout late 1992 and early 1993 a new stabilization package was implemented to fight hyperinflation. The new tax measures included higher customs duties, new business and hotel taxes, levies on petroleum, and an airport departure tax. The government also cut spending and as the new coalition took power in the latter half of 1993 revenue began to rise. The new Finance Minister Sam Rainsy also began to put in place measures aimed at eliminating "tax farming" and centralizing control over revenues. Under new laws passed by the Assembly, the national treasury began to gain control over tax coffers previously controlled by the provinces and ministries. In March 1994 Rainsy said that reform of the customs system and a revamp of budgetary procedures had so far increased revenues eight times. As a result the government was no longer printing money to fund the deficit.

Despite the progress, the budget situation is still vulnerable to a weak economy and military needs. The revenue system fails to tax entire sectors—including agriculture, which contributes 50 per cent of Cambodia's gross domestic product (GDP). Until spring 1994 there had also been no taxes on income or consumption. Import duties have made up 60 per cent of government revenue, hardly a sufficient basis for domestic funding programs. Military and civilian service salaries make up 60 per cent of current expenditures, leaving precious little to spend on social welfare programs and, most important to growth, capital expenditures.

Cambodia has little to export except rubber and timber. Modest amounts of maize, soybeans, sesame, and pepper are also exported. Tires constitute its only real manufactured product. It is difficult to determine the extent of illegal trade in cigarettes, alcohol, lumber, and gems. As far as imports, before 1991 Cambodia relied primarily on the Soviet Union for capital goods, machinery, heavy vehicles, oil, and cotton fabrics. Consumer imports were insignificant until the legion of UNTAC personnel arrived, spurring the purchase of vehicles, cameras, electronic goods, and air conditioners, much of it smuggled.

Despite the UNTAC surge, Cambodia's trade and current account deficits continue to rise. But recent reforms have begun to lay the groundwork for a modern trading economy. By mid-1993, the Ministry of Commerce had registered more than 500 trading companies, including five state-owned traders that handle major commodities like rubber, timber, rice, and fuel. In September of 1993 licensing regulations were eliminated on most commodities for trade by regis-tered companies and the port of Sihanoukville was opened to inter-national shipping. As a result of weak enforcement and low customs duties, Cambodia has become something of a regional hub for transit trade in the region, a development it can use to its advantage.

Before 1992 budget demands left little for public investment. But as the country began to stabilize, the international community began to carry out its pledges and investment rose from 9 to 15 per cent of GDP. Foreign savings, however, contributes most financing, and national savings remains a low 8 per cent that is not likely to change much in the short term.

Growth Prospects. Between 1991 and 1993, Cambodia's economy grew annually at 7–8 per cent and is now recovering from the slight sag of the uncertain election period a year ago. That high growth, however, was unbalanced and its impact limited. Expansion was largely due to UNTAC's effect on the service and construction industries, and to the surge in foreign investment catering to UNTAC's presence. It was centered in Phnom Penh, reaching only 15 per cent of the people; the city is now bustling with hotels, pizza parlors, computer shops, and hamburger joints called "McSams."

At least for the present all this is widening the gap in living standards between the urban and rural populations. Cambodia's agriculture sector accounts for more than half of its GDP and employs 80–85 per cent of its labor. Prosperity in Phnom Penh is important but it will not much improve Cambodia's chances for recovery. Nevertheless, the injection of substantial and properly targeted aid is expected to produce steady economic growth.

The World Bank has identified four principal goals for Cambodia's medium-term recovery: to maintain real growth rates of 7–8 per cent annually; to reduce inflation to a regional norm of 5 per cent (by 1995); to reduce the current account deficit eventually to 9 per cent of GDP (by 1996); and to raise international reserves. In the short term price stability and the growth of the private sector are politically and economically crucial.

Cambodia's growth potential makes the rehabilitation program all the more important. While industrial capacity is limited to agricultural subsectors, food production, tires, and building materials, the country is rich in arable land. If the critical task of mine clearance continues, food production will expand. Moreover, the growing demand of industrializing countries in Cambodia's region—for live-stock, rice, sugar, rubber, and other agricultural goods—offers real hope for increased exports.

In 1994 the production of energy and water supply will make up less than 1 per cent of Cambodian GDP—testimony to the Cambodians' poor standard of living. But that situation could rapidly improve with internationally assisted rehabilitation activities and development of agronomy. The discovery of oil or natural gas may also provide something of a bonanza and a real psychological boost. Several foreign companies are already drilling in the South China Sea, and substantial finds are predicted for 1994. Revenues of up to $300 million a year, which would transform Cambodia's prospects, are anticipated. The problem, of course, is that the gush of foreign exchange following an oil discovery would mostly benefit the corrupt and self-perpetuating elite of Phnom Penh.

Finally, despite UNTAC's departure, Cambodia's service sector can expect even higher rates of growth as the result of communications and transport improvements. Cambodia's potential for tourism is enor-mous if the international community can put to bed the horrific images of recent decades. The UNTAC presence has left a solid foundation, including hotels and restaurants, and ambitious plans have been laid for the restoration of the Angkor Wat ruins, which are in desperate need of protection from robbers who have stolen thousands of statues for sale on the international market. If security is guaranteed and transportation systems are improved, tourist prospects will be bright.

Rural Poverty. All economic statistics in Cambodia are suspect. However, some fundamental realities are obvious, and they bear on all plans for development.

- The population is growing at an extraordinarily rapid rate of 2.8 per cent per annum.
- More than half of the population is under 15, and the average Cambodian dies before reaching 50.
- More than half of Cambodian families are now headed by women. Many of the men who do head families are incapable of providing for their families' needs, often because of war wounds.

The traditional extended family support system has been destroyed.

Cambodia has virtually no family planning. On the contrary, the declaration of the Royal Government's policies issued to the National Assembly at the end of 1993 announced its intention "of increasing the number of Cambodians quickly" because the country "faces neighbors that have seven to eight times more people." But that racial imperative is likely to be counterproductive; a population that doubles in the next eighteen years (as Cambodia's will at present rates of growth) without massive accompanying investment would impoverish the country. Since no Cambodian government—now or before—has exhibited much interest in the plight of the deprived, farmers and their families flock to the cities hoping to work or beg.

Population growth is an important factor in economic growth, but Cambodia has a debilitated population. Many provinces have no health services whatsoever. In 1979 it was thought that just 43 physicians were left in Cambodia, and life expectancy was 31 years. Today, only about half the population has access to even the most rudimentary health services, and Cambodia's overall life expectancy is reckoned at 49.7 years. There is still a chronic shortage of doctors and of all medical services. One out of every eight children will die before his or her first birthday. Malaria is becoming more virulent throughout much of the country, and tuberculosis and dysentery are killing thousands. AIDS began to spread during the UNTAC period; it continues to do so.

In Cambodia the control of water is vital both to health and to agricultural life. International organizations have estimated that about 12 per cent of rural inhabitants and 20 per cent of city-dwellers have access to reliable drinking water. In some provinces UNICEF has been drilling wells in district centers. Often those wells provide the first groundwater sources and thus they greatly reduce health risks. The costs are minimal. In one province, Preah Vihear, 106 more wells are thought to be needed in villages, at an estimated cost of only $200,000. The returns on such an investment can be enormous. As for the irrigation so important to numerous crops, systems in many rural areas have simply broken down. Without monies for repair, boosting agricultural production will be difficult. Similarly, new electric power supplies are also badly needed; most of the countryside has none. Even in Phnom Penh the main electric generator (supplied by Czechoslovakia in the early 1980s) is close to the end of its working life.

Landmines. In Cambodia today there are estimated to be as many as 10 million mines. But almost half of those—perhaps 4.5 million—are laid as barrier minefields in remote, uninhabited border areas. They will have to be ignored.

The other 4 million or more are problem enough. They infect between 10 and 20 per cent of cultivated land and are killing or maiming nearly 300 people a month, mostly poor peasants between the ages of twenty-one and thirty-eight. Sadly, doctors must concentrate on amputations rather than on fighting tuberculosis, malaria, and other illnesses. Mine clearance is a priority.

UNTAC established the Cambodia Mine Action Center (CMAC), which provided equipment and training for Cambodian demining teams. Everyone assumed that UNTAC would donate the equipment when it left. But, to widespread consternation, in September 1993 UNTAC officials announced their intention of withdrawing the equipment. Ieng Mouly, the senior BLDP politician who had been put in charge of CMAC, warned that it would soon have to close. The United States, supported by such other countries as Sweden, then stepped in and bought the equipment for CMAC at a cost of $2.5 million.

Colonel George Focsaneau, the Canadian in charge of CMAC, was confident that the organization worked and that Cambodians could easily be trained to be deminers. "There is nothing magical about demining," he said. "It involves risk, of course, but it is not difficult. It just requires training, support and supervision." The problem is the funding. The costs are $10 million a year. That is a relatively small sum, but in recent months CMAC has survived only on a hand-to-mouth basis.

CMAC has an eight-year program to reduce mine casualties. The organization has trainers donated by Canada, Australia, New Zealand, and the Netherlands. But they must be retained and replaced on a rolling basis. They have already trained forty demining teams, fifty more teams to dispose of unexploded ordnance, and sixteen surveying teams. Demining is a painfully slow process that requires continued funding. By December 1993 only 19,000 mines had been cleared. For rural development to succeed in many areas, CMAC will need to be continually funded at least at the present level. In April 1994 demining in the northwest was stopped after the Khmer Rouge counterattacks in the area.

Roads. The landmine problem only exacerbates Cambodia's infrastructure problems. Over the last twenty-three years, Cambodia's basic structures have been so degraded that many of them are close to collapse. Cambodia has not invested in or repaired most of its infrastructure, and roads, water supplies, power links, schools, and hospitals barely exist or are hopelessly shattered.

Economy and infrastructure are interdependent. Without the physical capital, new industries cannot open and the market environment cannot expand. But until the economy is rejuvenated and roads open, rural poverty will increase, the gap between rural and urban incomes will continue to widen, and the infrastructure will continue to crumble.

The appalling state of Cambodia's roads, most of which were built in the 1920s and 1930s, is another case in point. It inhibits the flow of farm goods and commerce throughout the country. More than half of Cambodia's 3,000 kilometers of main roads—as well as many of its bridges—require repair and often complete rebuilding. It is easier and cheaper for inhabitants of outlying provinces to send their goods over the borders than to ship them to Phnom Penh. The isolation of Cambodian provinces continues to give the Khmer Rouge a better chance of increasing their influence. It also makes it hard for the central government to break down provincial warlordism.

For just one example, Route 7, which runs northeast from Kompong Cham through Snuol and Kratie to Stung Treng, once had a macadam surface for all its 363 kilometers. It is now passable only in the dry season, and its surface is so appalling that the journey takes three days instead of a few hours. Basic repairs to that one road would open a large part of the country to the government and to commerce; it would cost only an estimated $10 million.

Most ongoing projects from the UNTAC period have been aimed at restoring roads and bridges to minimally traversable conditions to meet immediate, short term needs. In 1994 reconstruction programs should be geared to improvements of a more permanent nature, including paving roadways to withstand weather and long-term traffic and strengthening bridges to withstand erosion and flood. Efforts must also focus on extending programs designed to link rural roads and rehabilitated highways. That type of assistance is crucial for integrating Cambodia's agricultural markets; funding by the United Nations Development Program (UNDP) and bilateral donors will, unfortunately, expire in 1994.

Public Sector. Currently, the Cambodian civil service employs about 147,000 personnel, or 1.7 per cent of the population—almost double what is usually considered the appropriate proportion for a developing country, let alone for a government that has ceased to perform many of the traditional functions of government. That size reflects in part the command and control economy installed by the Vietnamese but mostly the vast, thinly spread system of patronage through which ordinary Cambodians tapped the state apparatus as a social security net.

The conundrum is how to ensure a transition to a structure of government that fulfills the Paris Agreement, is in tune with Cambodian political realities, and provides real services to the public. By mid-1993 civil servants and health workers were so desperately poor that they were selling off their office furniture and the small stocks of drugs remaining in the hospitals. Some UNTAC offices in the provinces were looted as soon as UNTAC officials withdrew.

Transition is probably harder in Cambodia than in most former communist countries. While the ideology of previous regimes is being discarded, government functions must be redefined and made more effective. Central authority also needs a national reach; the warlordism of the provinces has to be replaced by regional government actually responsive to the center.

There is virtually no legislative framework governing the civil service. Basic service reforms will have to establish and strengthen professional cadres with recognized salary levels, scales, and incentives. Cadres must be taught to serve not the CPP, or any party, but the nation; that will take years.

In most ministries, not surprisingly, it has proved hard to change the structure and patterns of overemployment and underpayment established over a decade by the CPP, even where a FUNCINPEC minister is now in charge. Thus the Minister of Industry, a Khmer who worked until recently for Boeing in Seattle, brought friends and assistants with him. But they have responsibilities and families in the United States and find it impossible to live on $30 a month. Such salaries are open invitations to either departure or corruption. There are 450 employees in the Industry Ministry itself and another 4,500 working in plants associated with the ministry throughout the country. The Minister recognizes that complete civil service reform is needed. "We need to give job security for real jobs. People find it hard to understand that we have to move away from a centrally planned economy."

Finance Minister Rainsy has proposed a solution for the civil service. It is to choose, preferably by competition, some 50,000 people out of the present 130,000 and to fashion them into an elite corps to be paid a living salary of perhaps $200 a month. The remainder would be retained at their present salaries—in effect, pensions—until the expanding private sector could pick them up. Such radical restructuring could not be achieved quickly. It would have to be carried out ministry by ministry, itself a huge problem. The CPP and its cadres will inevitably resist any such moves, and the success of the restructuring would be contingent on the development of the whole economy.

Indeed, since the beginning of 1994, Rainsy has been under increasing attack for many of these and other radical measures that threaten to upset vested and often corrupt interests in the country. His proposals have won him widespread public support, but he enjoys little within the government. After Prime Ministers Ranariddh and Hun Sen failed to persuade the king to remove him from office, Ranariddh went on state television to attack Rainsy (without naming him) for "demagoguery." As of this writing Rainsy's position is still uncertain. That very fact undermines confidence in the government's intent to confront the country's problems.

Education. Even if Cambodia had the money to reform itself, the society is bereft of qualified institutions and individuals. Although Cambodia concentrated on building up its primary school system in the 1950s and later its secondary and tertiary institutions, education began to collapse during the war. In the Khmer Rouge period many of those with education and training were deliberately put to death; intellectual life was virtually eliminated. Because so few masons, carpenters, electricians, plumbers, or other kinds of artisans have been reared in Cambodia, the country has become dependent upon Vietnamese workers, adding to already fierce ethnic tensions.

The government of the People's Republic of Kampuchea (later the State of Cambodia) did attempt to rebuild the system. Owing to the large number of adult illiterates and the disruption of schooling in the 1970s, the government placed priority on primary education. By 1992 about 300,000 students were thought to be enrolled in lower secondary education and 5,000 in upper secondary. But many were trained in Russian or Vietnamese language, while English and French are now the foreign languages of choice in Cambodia.

In rural areas where the state education system has not been fully restarted, children get little or no education. The dropout rate in primary schools is around 50 per cent, and only about 35–40 per cent of children who graduate from primary school continue to secondary school. Even when a basic structure exists at the primary level, children aged six to twelve often attend school for only three or four days a month—and many do not attend at all. Adult literacy is about 35 per cent and little is being done to improve it.

UNESCO has tried to strengthen the community temple learning centers in rural Cambodia. Until the French reduced the role of those community temples—and the Khmer Rouge eliminated them altogether—they had served as learning centers for the Khmer people. Monks and other members of the local intelligentsia transmitted basic literacy and Buddhist ethics, a wide range of cultural and

economic skills, and local folk knowledge. The subjects included arts
and crafts, vernacular architecture and construction techniques, sus-
tainable agriculture and forestry, traditional medicine, music and
performing arts, and even astronomy.

In recent years monastic service has been reintroduced, and temples
have been restored. UNESCO's pilot project in Battambang illustrated
the potential of the temples. In one village of 400 families, 400 people
signed up for a course in basic literacy and traditional construction
techniques being offered at a temple. Village elders and skilled workers
do not hesitate to offer their services as informal teachers.

International Assistance. Foreign investors avoid Cambodia for a
variety of sound reasons: the degradation of the physical capital and
the absence of infrastructure; the uncertain consequences of Cambodia's rapidly growing population; a small consumer market; the poor
natural resource base; corruption; and civil disorder. Moreover, the
country lacks any legislation that offers security to investors.

While over time foreign investment may ultimately be forthcom-
ing, Cambodia needs immediate help that can only come from
public sources. International assistance is necessary simply to support
rehabilitation activities and finance the budget deficit. (External aid
currently makes up half of the Cambodian budget.)

A spring 1994 World Bank report on Cambodia stressed that
success in rehabilitation "will depend heavily on enhancing community participation; developing human resources; strengthening institutions; improving investment programming; providing well-tar-
geted technical assistance; and improving security." The Bank also
underscores the importance of consultation among the major donors
to avoid duplicating efforts. So far the record has been good and
U.N. organizations and NGOs have worked well together with bilateral donors to maximize public assistance while encouraging govern-
ment-sponsored programs.

In April 1992 the U.N. secretary-general launched a consolidated
appeal for Cambodia's immediate needs and national rehabilitation,
as required by the Paris Peace Agreement. He requested $595 million
to address repatriation, food security, health, water, housing, training, and education. Some $150 million was to go toward the repair

of transport utilities, and $126 million was to be devoted to public-sector financing. A May 1992 assessment of Cambodia's "Socio-Economic Situation and Immediate Needs" summed up the importance of that aid: "Without significant outside help Cambodia stands a very real chance of regression and a return to social, economic and political turmoil."

When the donor nations met in Tokyo in June 1992, they responded generously and pledged $880 million. However, pledges were swifter than actual disbursement. Much of the money is still uncommitted. Those pledges need to be unlocked and disbursed. Many pledges were also earmarked for long-term development projects rather than for immediate rehabilitation needs. But the country's low absorptive capacity is often a constraint.

Until now Cambodian appeals have met with positive responses. Donor countries have also pledged to pay off Cambodia's $52 million overdue debts to the International Monetary Fund (IMF). The UNDP coordinates some technical assistance programs in Cambodia, including general planning, project preparation, statistical systems development, macro-economic management, fiscal and monetary policy, and taxation. Foreign advisers aid the National Bank, the Ministry of Finance, and the Ministry of Planning; and the UNDP has also sent an environmental advisory team for eighteen months.

While donors tend to respond quickly to large, visible humanitarian assistance projects, small-scale village projects attract less attention but probably do more to generate confidence and employment and improve life. UNTAC produced a list of 150 small-scale projects in thirteen difference provinces. Their total cost is about $7.2 million. Some individual projects cost as little as $5,000. Most are still waiting to be implemented. UNHCR has also developed so-called Quick-Impact Projects (QIPs) in an attempt to improve the infrastructure so that the 360,000 repatriated refugees stand a better chance of being reintegrated into their communities. As of March 1993 UNHCR had funded 49 projects worth $5.5 million, including the repair of 218.5 kilometers of tertiary roads, 209 schools, 1,150 water projects, and 21 health centers. Although QIPs are expensive, they may prove cost effective by highlighting the immediate returns from the election.

The most recent tranche of international assistance was unlocked at the second annual meeting of the International Committee of the Reconstruction of Cambodia (ICORC), convened in Tokyo in March 1994. Prince Ranariddh, speaking for himself and Hun Sen, read a statement from King Sihanouk calling for a "Marshall Plan" for Cambodia. He said that without UNTAC disarmament of the Khmer Rouge, the Royal Cambodian Government had inherited an insecure situation for which it must find the "most appropriate" solution. He spoke of the overriding need for reform in the introduction of the new investment code and a decision to decrease spending on defense and increase funding for education. Even so, security spending would still absorb close to a third of the government's 1994 budget of $350 million.

Underlining the American future interest in Cambodia, Secretary of State Warren Christopher attended the Tokyo meeting. He pronounced Cambodia's transformation over the past year as one of the most remarkable anywhere. The success of the May 1993 election gave hope that the peace would last; he remarked that those who said democracy was a Western contrivance had forgotten to tell the Cambodian people. He hoped that with further international assistance, Cambodia would join the "new Pacific community" for which President Clinton had called.

The final pledge for 1994 was a little more than $500 million, including nearly $16 million for demining. The principal bilateral donors were Japan ($91.8 million), France ($40 million), and the U.S. ($33.3 million). The Asian Development Bank and the IMF pledged a total of $196 million. Vietnam offered to provide services for Cambodian reconstruction to facilitate trade shipments and transport through Vietnam. The donor conference brought the total of funds committed to the country since 1991 to $1.7 billion.

However, the recorded pledges in fact overstated the amounts actually spent or available. They included bilateral pledges already made but not yet disbursed and some projects that were feasible but not necessarily to be committed for this year. The real total of pledges was probably nearer to $300 million than to $500 million, but even that was an important demonstration of continuing support for Cambodia.

The bottom line is that in 1993 Cambodians voted for both peace and a chance to improve their lives. The potential is there. The question now is whether internal and external resources can be deployed effectively both to resuscitate the country and to develop its capacity to manage and sustain its own development. The World Bank has pointed out that institutional constraints and a lack of qualified people mean that the rehabilitation programs are proceeding more slowly than expected. "It should therefore be emphasized," warned the Bank, "that rebuilding the economy and reconstructing the physical capital ravaged by two decades of conflict will take many years."

Epilogue: The Problems One Year On

At the end of May 1994, there was writing on the walls of Phnom Penh. The words were ghostly but chilling. Over and over again they appeared, as both a threat and a warning: LON NOL, LON NOL, LON NOL.

Exactly one year after the people made their stunning, good-tempered request for changed and better lives, Cambodia seemed at times to bear a startling resemblance to the early 1970s when corrupt generals of the Lon Nol regime sold American-supplied arms to the Khmer Rouge and sent untrained, unpaid boys to fight them. In mid-1994 much the same sort of thing is happening again.

Last time the Khmer Rouge won. While a repeat victory is not now in sight and Cambodia still has far greater opportunities today than it did twenty years ago, the portents are depressing. Disarray, drift, corruption, factionalism, military negligence, and naivete—all recall the catastrophic later years of the Lon Nol regime. The government needs to get serious.

The immediate cause of the disarray was the string of serious military defeats that the government suffered in its attacks upon the Khmer Rouge in Anlong Veng and Pailin. The crisis of confidence that the losses had caused both at home and abroad seemed at times to be shaking the very basis of the Paris Agreement and the government that was created as a result of the UNTAC elections.

The stories from the attack on Pailin were indeed terrifying. "Generals" of the Royal Cambodian Army went around spray painting their names on doors of the houses they were each planning to loot, or where they intended to install their mistresses. Many of the officers were drunk when a handful of Khmer Rouge counterattacked. The unpaid and wretched government soldiers fled and the Khmer Rouge advanced almost to the outskirts of Cambodia's second city, Battambang. They have not yet been driven all the way back and their lines are further east into Cambodia than at any time since the Vietnamese overthrew them in 1979.

In villages they have occupied, they have reconfirmed their bloody reputation, killing villagers and burning houses. Both sides have decapitated prisoners—so far the Royal Army more than the Khmer Rouge. In parts of the northwest close to the Thai border, roads that had been rebuilt have been cut, bridges that were reconstructed have been been blown up, and schools that were rebuilt have been burned down. In short, the situation is worse than at any time in the last five years.

The fighting and destruction have had an appalling effect on confidence amongst both foreign investors and tourists. In April and May 1994, government receipts from all sources dropped by as much as 50 per cent. A huge power project in Phnom Penh is now having trouble finding investors. One estimate is that the country has lost two years' development in just a few weeks. And yet even this setback has not seemed to have instilled a sense of urgency in the government or the armed forces. In a brief visit at the end of May, this writer sensed that drift, indecision, and complacency are still the order of the day. Equally remarkable (though, in the circumstances, understandable) has been a falling away of sympathy for Cambodia amongst international organizations and Western embassies that till now have been pressing Cambodia's case. For the first time, foreign diplomats and aid officials are expressing impatience.

One foreign aid official recalled that a few weeks earlier, the traffic in Phnom Penh at the funeral of General Saksutsakhan had stretched around the block. Almost every car seemed to be a Mercedes. And almost every one appeared to belong to a general. As already mentioned, there are now 2,000 generals in the Cambodian army and 10,000 colonels. Many of these "officers" are not even soldiers; they bought their stripes to be able to intimidate and extort more effectively.

The nominal payroll of the entire army has now increased from the 128,000 registered by UNTAC's Operation Paymaster to close to 160,000 today—eight or ten times the ideal size of the army. But many of these soldiers, as in the Lon Nol days, are "phantoms," whose pay is pocketed by officers. The army is corrupt through and through. When officers want ammunition, they often have to buy it from officials of the CPP. And those same officers often resell it to the Khmer Rouge. The debacle at Pailin was the catastrophic result.

Corruption is everywhere. School diplomas have to be bought, as does even the rudimentary medical care that is supposed to be free. In Phnom Penh's new rush hour scores of policemen shake down every motorist and motorcycle driver. Deals and kickbacks define contractual obligations. The head of one international agency said that he was horrified by what he now sees. "It's just the pie. They are all grabbing as big a share as they can."

Some senior Cambodian officials are also alarmed by the corruption. One said, "These businessmen are so terrible. They just offer bribes, bribes, bribes. One of them left a gold ingot on my desk. I told him to take it away but he would not. What could I do?" A leading Australian official who visited Phnom Penh in May listened to requests for assistance from Cambodia's military. He responded with some asperity that the donors had needs too: they needed to see a small, uncorrupt army in which generals were honest and soldiers were trained and paid properly. The generals were taken aback, but they can expect more such responses. One French diplomat said, "I am really impatient with them now. I have told them they cannot have arms. We need to know what is their idea of an army. They never listen; they are increasing the size of the army instead of reducing it."

International aid officials of all sorts are beginning to reconsider their future investments in Cambodia. In Washington, officials of the World Bank speak of a government in Phnom Penh that is ignoring the realities. The problem of working with the government is that it often has the effect of exacerbating existing power rivalries and aiding factions that have in truth demonstrated little interest in solving the nation's problems.

* * *

It was inevitable that there would be a backlash. The election of
May 1993 was so magnificent an event that some of the expectations
it aroused amongst both foreigners and Cambodians were unrealistic.
Cambodia is not only a formerly communist state attempting to
move to a market economy; it is also afflicted by the problems of
extreme poverty, an undeveloped political class, and the Khmer Rouge.
When the Royal Government was finally formed and the constitution
was adopted in fall 1993, the last twenty-three years of civil war and
political and economic decline—preceded by decades of court
intrigues and political stasis—were all on the table. Any government
would have had trouble dealing with such handicaps, even had it
not been a deadlocked coalition.

There have been many significant achievements since, as stated
in the preceding pages. Cambodia is still a far more open country with
many more freedoms than it was before UNTAC. There is a flourishing
independent press—though it is under some threat now. Human
rights are respected—not perfectly, but better now than ever before.

The Minister for Rural Development, Dr. Huot, has inspired confidence amongst aid officials; he is attempting to get training started
and appears to see the urgency to reach into the provinces as quickly
as possible. But so long as both prime ministers show inadequate
concern and so long as the military consumes such a huge share of
resources, his and other essential social ministries will be starved.
On the other hand, the Secretariat for Women's Affairs (run by a
man) appears to have made a good start.

Driving through some parts of the countryside, one sees many more
houses with tiled roofs. The market sector is growing all the time.
But many other areas are still steeped in poverty and have felt no
change since the election. Efficient economic programs continue
in different provinces. The World Food Program (WFP) has 830 food-
for-work schemes in villages, and many of them are helping. Many
NGOs are doing similarly effective, small-scale, often unseen work.
WFP officials say "muddling through" may be the answer, and it is
certainly better than collapse.

Conversely, the new fighting has created at least 50,000 new inter-
nally displaced people, and the levels of hardship for those whom

UNHCR bussed back from the border in 1992–93 is rising. Up to 30 per cent of them have no land and no jobs; they are destitute, and their predicament will get worse until the government addresses the needs of the bulk of the people—the peasantry—seriously.

The source of most problems is political—namely deadlock in the coalition. Issues are dealt with first and foremost on a political basis, with technical considerations secondary. Factionalism becomes ever more extreme. The CPP is now split between the Hun Sen wing and that of Chea Sim, the President of the National Assembly. It is not always possible to predict which will be the more "liberal" or reactionary on any given issue. There are similar schisms in FUNCIN-PEC: Ranariddh has become disenchanted with Sam Rainsy and with his uncle Sirivudh, the Foreign Minister—and they with him. The king seems enchanted with no one.

Each government leader seems eager to blame his failures on others. UNTAC comes in for widespread, if facile, attack. It is true that the U.N.'s failure to demobilize and disarm the combatants, or to take control of the key ministries of the State of Cambodia, meant that the coalition compromise was the most that FUNCINPEC could wrest from its election victory. FUNCINPEC's inability to assume power after the election has induced a state of deadlock, in which the CPP still controls the army, the police, and much of the administration. "We have inherited from UNTAC a demobilisation of spirit," complained Ranariddh to the *Far Eastern Economic Review*. But to many observers the problem is that Ranariddh himself has done little to counter that demobilization by asserting firm leadership or even enunciating any vision for the country. That in the end is the real issue.

Prince Ranariddh sometimes appears unable to concentrate on issues for any length of time. His critics believe he is happy with the trappings of power and unwilling to fight for the substance. In May a senior foreign mine clearance official was astounded when the prime minister kept him for two hours to talk about motor cars. Ranariddh spent the best part of one May afternoon lecturing architecture students about the design of parks in Phnom Penh—one of his priorities. Often Ranariddh seems to have surrendered real power to his co-prime minister, Hun Sen.

Hun Sen seems to some foreign officials in Phnom Penh to be a more serious politician than Ranariddh, but he is still locked into the intrigues, power struggles, and corruption of the CPP. He too has failed to set a defined political agenda for the nation. But his influence over Ranariddh seems to grow apace. Ranariddh's critics within his own party think that it was madness for FUNCINPEC to agree to the CPP's demands that the Royal Cambodian Armed Forces attack the Khmer Rouge in Anlong Veng and Pailin. FUN-CINPEC was elected in the hope and on the promise of peace, not further war.

One senior FUNCINPEC official expressed a most pessimistic view, saying, "We have been swallowed and digested by the CPP. We were elected by the people to bring peace and development. Instead we have been pushed into adopting all the CPP's policies, including attacking the Khmer Rouge. Both the CPP and the Khmer Rouge need the war. The CPP have stopped us keeping any of our promises. Sometimes I think that all aid should be stopped. There is no point in giving analgesics when surgery is required."

Amongst ministries, Finance is still seen as the greatest success by donors. Sam Rainsy's achievements, described above, are significant but the struggle for financial reform is an uphill one. He has managed to stabilize the currency, control inflation, and raise the tax revenues of the government. But he has two problems. He has to constantly fight the CPP's resistance to change, and it has become clear that he is at odds with Ranariddh, who appears to dislike the praise the international community has given his minister of finance. Ranariddh has openly dismissed him as "our own Zorro" or "Robin Hood."

For his part, Rainsy has made no secret of his belief that FUNCINPEC has done far too little to stand up to CPP bullying and corrupt practices. Rainsy's largest problem (and that of the country) is the huge cost of the army. The Minister of Finance has no power to question any of the army's demands for funds; he has to sign any invoice he is presented. World Bank officials in Washington say that unless this practice is ended soon, and overall military costs are cut back, the economy can never recover.

No restraint on the executive is coming from the National Assembly, which continues to disappoint. Few members of the Assembly ever go to their constituencies; most are more interested in spending their enormous salaries in Phnom Penh or even abroad. Too many of FUNCINPEC's people are more involved in court intrigues than in national politics. No questions were asked in the Assembly about the military's defeat at Pailin.

In April and May the National Assembly finally started discussing legislation. But the bellwether investment code was postponed again and again because of disagreements. Equally important—and disturbing—is the press bill. The punitive and restrictive legislation that the government proposed was withdrawn in May for further review, after international anti-censorship groups like Article 19 and Asia Watch protested.

At the end of May, the Minister of Information, Ieng Mouly, said that he hoped to liberalize the bill but was still uncertain whether the Council of Ministers would accept it. Amongst the clauses that had excited most criticism were those that empowered ministers to unilaterally deny information to the media; enabled the Ministry to close down any publication on the grounds of a threat to national defense or public order; stated that truth was no defense against defamation suits; and restricted the sale of books. The extent and success of the amendments was not clear by early June. Some senior FUNCINPEC ministers, including Ranariddh, were reported to be even more keen than those from the CPP to muzzle the press. If they succeed, there will be no check whatsoever on abuse of power by the authorities and by commercial interests. The press law remains a serious test of the government's good faith and adherence to the promise of the constitution.

As this report went to press, the threat to the press looked more grim than ever. On June 11, Tou Chhom Mongkol, the editor-in-chief of the newspaper *Antarakhum* (*Intervention*) died of a fractured skull. He had been attacked on Monivong Boulevard, one of the main streets of the city, and had suffered a single blow to his head. The motive was not robbery, for his motorcycle lay beside him, undamaged. *Antarakhum* is a bi-weekly paper that has published articles critical of leaders of both parties. In March 1994 a grenade was thrown by two men on a motorbike into its office; the explosion wounded five persons. No one was arrested and no police report was ever made public. The murder of Tou Chhom Mongkol took place at a time when the press was coming under increasing harassment from government security officials. In recent weeks three newspapers have been ordered to cease publication after printing articles critical of the government. Foreign journalists have been threatened with expulsion because of "negative reporting."

King Sihanouk's political statements have been no less confusing. After apparently successful treatment for his cancer, the king spent six weeks in the country in April and May sowing confusion amongst different members of the government; no one was quite certain what he wanted. He seemed at various times to support military attacks upon the Khmer Rouge, and to wish to see the movement outlawed. At other times, he worked diligently to set up "round table" talks in which the Khmer Rouge would participate. He even invited the Khmer Rouge leader, Khieu Samphan, to sleep at the palace to guarantee his safety in Phnom Penh. Khieu Samphan refused.

In one press conference the king lamented that Cambodia was finished; he attacked the government, FUNCINPEC, and his own family for their internal bickering; he warned that the disunity could lead to the return of the Khmer Rouge, whom he described as wishing to return Cambodia to the Stone Age. "There is civil war between the Khmer Rouge and the royal armed forces, civil war within FUNCINPEC, civil war everywhere," he said. He apologized to the United Nations and said that Cambodia did not deserve the U.N. elections.

The king seemed to equate the government and the Khmer Rouge as similar nuisances, as if each were equally disobedient and unruly children whom only he could discipline. Hun Sen told ambassadors that he felt undermined. Ranariddh revealed that he too felt estranged from his father. But in one sense the king was correct. The government and particularly its two prime ministers were failing the country.

While he was in Phnom Penh, members of his court and what one could call "the king's party" urged that he be given extraordinary powers to rule the country and not merely reign. They recalled that in the early 1950s he was given exceptional powers and a three-year mandate to gain independence from France—which he did successfully. But today the implication would be much more serious: it would mean that the country's carefully won democratic constitution would be abandoned.

Demonstrations demanding special powers for him were arranged by his supporters for May 17, and then called off when it seemed that they would provoke counter-demonstrations and violence. Whether the king himself wanted to be asked to assume total powers remained ambiguous. The king left Phnom Penh in mid-May to return to Beijing for medical treatment. The Khmer Rouge then agreed to meet with the government, under Sihanouk's auspices, in North Korea at the end of May. Dozens of senior officials flew out of Phnom Penh on different planes and by different routes to Pyongyang. It was a waste of time and money. The talks failed and the Khmer Rouge threat loomed larger.

Khmer Rouge strength is, as ever, disputed; reasonable estimates vary between 6,000 and 10,000. Whatever their numbers, they can afford to take a long view. They demonstrate extraordinary tenacity. They keep the villages they control in an information vacuum, which the government does little to fill. Government-controlled radio and television programming is too often propagandistic and dishonest. The integrity and skill of Radio UNTAC is much missed.

After the Pailin debacle the Khmer Rouge seem to have embarked on a new strategy of political and military attacks upon the government. They appear to have decided that Ranariddh has fallen completely under the control of Hun Sen and the CPP and that as a result they will never be offered any real representation in the coalition. A Khmer Rouge communiqué dated May 5 stated: "Up to now Hun Sen and Ranariddh have not expressed any intention of compromising. So unfortunately, we are obliged to push more on the battlefield to convince them they will not get anything more by military means."

The Khmer Rouge are, once again, developing support amongst students in the towns. One Western ambassador was horrified in May to meet a group of highly intelligent students in Phnom Penh who told him that FUNCINPEC had come to power with a mandate for three things: To get rid of the Vietnamese, to protect the borders, and to root out corruption. The government had failed at all three, and for that reason the Khmer Rouge were needed back in Phnom Penh to clean up the mess. These young people had no real memories of Khmer Rouge atrocities—their youth had been defined by the Vietnamese occupation and for most of them distaste for Vietnam was a much more important emotion. When the ambassador reminded them that the Khmer Rouge were responsible for the deaths of at least hundreds of thousands of Cambodians, they replied that this was government propaganda that could not be trusted. At present the Khmer Rouge cannot be beaten. They can and should be contained.

The Cambodian government's principal wounds are self-inflicted, but there is no doubt that other serious blows are being administered by the continuing covert, yet blatant, assistance given by Thai military officers to the Khmer Rouge. And direct evidence exists—such as photographs of Thai officers working closely with their Khmer Rouge counterparts. If the Thais had declined to repatriate the groups of Khmer Rouge soldiers and families who fled from the government's initial attack on Pailin, they would have deprived the Khmer Rouge of a substantial part of their fighting force. Instead, they sent them back to fight another day, giving the civilians no chance of escape. Furthermore, the Thai government still refuses to hand over weapons FUNCINPEC had received from China before the Paris Agreement and that had been stored in Thailand, on the grounds that Thailand is "neutral." Meanwhile, Thai officers produce weapons and logistical support for their Khmer Rouge business partners.

The underlying truth is that a weak Cambodia has, for many years, been an ambition of Thai foreign policy. The problem is how best to deal with the Thais. The denunciations of Thailand by Cambodia's leaders have become fiercer and louder—and perhaps more counterproductive. They have had the effect of lining up the weak civilian Thai government with the military. It is sometimes more fruitful to entice and attract Thailand than to denounce it.

The Thai government continually claims that it cannot control its military along the border. International sanctions will never be imposed on Thailand, a key regional player and ally of the West. But attempts should be made to convince the Thais—including the military—that they have much more to gain from close commercial and political relations with Phnom Penh than from commerce with the border warlords.

ASEAN should also get involved. It, after all, played the crucial diplomatic role in isolating Vietnam during its ten-year occupation. ASEAN's interest in Cambodia seems to have been diminished since the Paris Peace Agreement. The U.S. and other Western allies need to refocus the organization's attention on the problem. The partners should put all possible pressure on Thailand to break its links with the Khmer Rouge. And the early admission of both Cambodia and Vietnam into the association should be negotiated.

* * *

Since the end of the 1970s, Cambodia's suffering has captured the attention of the Western world. Feelings of shame and responsibility for the way in which war engulfed the country in the 1970s were aroused by the successful feature film *The Killing Fields* and by countless documentaries showing mass graves and prison torture chambers, refugees on apparently endless marches, and ceaseless factional warring.

But defining the realities of Cambodia has always been difficult. As in many other crises, soundbites and quick-fix cliches have controlled our perceptions. Piles of skulls and charges of "Asian Hitlers" have been overlaid with the outdated rhetoric of the Vietnam War.

The Paris Peace Agreement took place in part because what is called "the international community" considered that it had a debt to Cambodia. Against huge odds the agreement was successful—not wholly, but enough to give Cambodia a chance. Now the terrifying possibility emerges that the opportunity will be lost.

The areas of need indicated in this report are not intended to be conclusive or comprehensive. Every Cambodian and every foreign expert will list different Cambodian needs in a different order of priority. It bears repetition to say that on the wish list (not necessarily in order of importance) are peace with the Khmer Rouge, demobilization, civil service reform, a judicial system, law and order, human rights, guarantees for a free press, mine clearance, rural development, credit, health services, education, the return of skilled Cambodians from overseas, an anticorruption drive, repairs to infrastructure, new industry, a customs service, and revenue collection—and that is just to start.

Underlying all other problems is the lack of effective political will. Prince Ranariddh has complained that Cambodia is being abandoned. In particular, he and other leaders have complained that they are being left to fight the Khmer Rouge without weapons. No one, he claims, will even sell the Cambodians ammunition. Phnom Penh had ordered Chinese ammunition through a Singapore company, but the Chinese government blocked the sale. Ranariddh said they had even tried to buy ammunition from Vietnam, but Hanoi had refused.

Given the disgraceful nature of the Cambodian army, international reluctance is understandable. By the end of May a consensus appears to have begun to grow amongst principal donors and supporters of the Royal Government—in particular the United States, France, and Australia—that while Cambodia needs help, it would be catastrophic to pour weaponry into and onto the present military structures. As in the Lon Nol years, vast quantities of it would end up being sold to the Khmer Rouge or to the Thais and little improvement would be made in the army's competence.

The present armed forces cannot defeat the Khmer Rouge, and they should not be given any encouragement to try. A far better course is for the government merely to try and contain the Khmer Rouge within the areas they control and to build up the economy of the great majority of the country, which remains in government

hands. Any military assistance must be tied to radical reform and
reduction of the armed forces. Without this reduction, military assistance will aggravate the present problems. But it remains a real question
whether the present government has the political will to reduce the
army or convert fighting troops into engineering battalions.

At the moment international financial institutions face a real
dilemma: how long can they continue to provide budget support—
which is designed to provide counterpart funds for bilateral donors'
capital projects and to create the necessary framework for economic
stability—when about half the aid is being squandered on fruitless
military operations? The military adventurism of early 1994, and
the subsequent defeats, have terrifying economic implications and
there is now a real fear that inflation and exchange rate instability
could return again.

Sometimes it seemed that only the king was possessed by a sense
of urgency. In the middle of June Sihanouk caused further consternation when, in Beijing, he told Nate Thayer of the *Phnom Penh Post*
that he was under great pressure to "seize power." This would amount
to an attempt at a constitutional coup, though he stressed that it
could only happen if, as the constitution allows, two-thirds of the
Assembly voted to give him "extraordinary" powers.

The king said his plan was to be his own prime minister and head
of state. He would have four vice presidents: Ranariddh, Hun Sen,
Sirivudh, and Sam Rainsy. His program would be one of national
reconciliation and as such he intended to give "important portfolios"
to the Khmer Rouge. He described the program as "the rehabilitation
and reconstruction of the country," saying that "the only difference
I will make is a radical change in my non-war policy. No war with
the Khmer Rouge and the Khmer Rouge in my government. It is
the only change! The only change! But it is the very, very basis of
my process of saving Cambodia."

He insisted that he would maintain the liberty of the press. "They
can criticize me! I will not let them have a pretext to condemn me
as a dictator or a putschist." He said he realized that it would be
impossible for him to do anything unless he had the support of Hun

Sen and the CPP's security services. "I do not want to shed blood to fight a secession led by Hun Sen. . . .I need Hun Sen. I need his support." As for Ranariddh, the king said, "I am sure that my son will not betray me. . . .He will accept certainly. Not with joy. With sadness certainly. With anger certainly. But he will, I am sure, not rebel."

The king perhaps does understand—and ministers from all parties need to—that in the world beyond Cambodia donor fatigue is a very real condition. Many of those most enthusiastic about helping Cambodia have finite resources—of both patience and money— and there are many other areas of the world that command greater attention, for obvious and often good reasons. Russia and the Middle East are consuming more and more U.S. resources. The peoples of Rwanda, Haiti, Somalia, Bosnia, Burundi, and many other places are suffering more now than the Cambodians. Cambodian ministers, especially the two prime ministers, must understand that the world does not owe them a living. Long-term international interest and application will always be needed to follow up peacekeeping efforts, but it cannot be unconditional.

If the government does not learn from the lessons of Lon Nol, stamp out corrupt factionalism, and implement genuine reforms, the conditions of ordinary people will not improve and the appeal of the Khmer Rouge will grow. Young people, who do not remember the Khmer Rouge terror and who loathe the depravity the regime has failed to halt, will become attracted. Disillusionment will spread even among the brave peasants who defied all intimidation in May 1993 to vote for change. The Cambodian people deserve better than what they have so far been given.

Cambodia is Cambodian now. The success of its new deal lies principally with the duly elected government. But the international community did not deliver on all of its promises; it still bears a responsibility towards the country. Cambodia will need financial and technical assistance for a long time. But above all it needs good governance. It has had some in recent months, but not nearly enough. The donors must impress upon the Royal Cambodian Government that corruption, drift, and lack of cooperation are insupportable. The international community has both the right and the duty to insist that the Cambodian government make every effort to fulfill the promises of the historic election that the world brought to Cambodia.

Sources and
Acknowledgements

Cambodia's New Deal is dedicated to my daughter Ellie. The material for the report was collected on seven visits to Cambodia in 1992 and 1993. I traveled to different parts of the country and spoke to scores of people. I am grateful to His Majesty King Norodom Sihanouk for giving me his unique perspective. Amongst others who were very helpful were His Royal Highness Prince Norodom Ranariddh; Second Prime Minister Hun Sen; H.E. Son Sann; Foreign Minister Norodom Sirivudh; Finance Minister Sam Rainsy; Information Minister Ieng Mouly; Tioulong Saumura, Deputy Governor of the National Bank; Deputy Information Minister Khieu Kanariddh; Truong Mealy; Madame Kek Sisoda; Roland Eng; Sina Than; Uch Kim An; Veng Sereyvuth; and Penn Thol.

Within UNTAC and the United Nations, many people assisted me. They included H.E. Yasushi Akashi, Lieutenant General John Sanderson, Reg Austin, Tim Carney, Sergio Vieira de Mello, Dennis MacNamara, Michael Williams, Michael Ward, Steve Heder, Isabelle Abric, Jay Carter, Nicki Dahrendorf, Peter Barthu, Russell Stewart, Peter Swarbrick, Mary Fisk, Eric Falt, Christophe Peschoux, Judy Ledgerwood, Setsuko Miyaji, Scott Leiper, and Andrew Ladley.

At the U.S. Mission, Ambassador Charles Twining and Mark Storella gave all assistance. David Burns, the British Ambassador, and Inger Burns were unfailingly supportive and knowledgeable. Australian officials including Foreign Minister Gareth Evans, Ambassador John Holloway, and Nick Warner were all most helpful. So was Edouard Wattez of the U.N. Development Program.

Amongst the press corps, NGOs, and other friends, I would like to thank Sochua Mu Leiper, Julio Jeldres, Sue Downie, Ravynn Karet-Coxen, Nate Thayer, Michael Hayes, Kathleen Hayes, Marie Augier, Sue Aitkin, Mary-Kay Magistad, Elizabeth Becker, Ed Fitzgerald, Tan Sotho, Carol Livingston, Matthew Middlemiss, David Chandler, Jules Thomas, Karen Emmons, and Tim Page, whose magnificent photograph forms the cover of this book. I have quoted extensively from the *Phnom Penh Post*, especially for events in early 1994; it is an excellent newspaper.

At the Carnegie Endowment, I would like to thank its President, Morton Abramowitz, who had the original idea for this report, and Betsy Hamilton, Samantha Power, and Lukas Haynes for all the time and trouble they put into it.

William Shawcross
London
June 1994